"This Practical Powerful Proph[e] hoping to walk close to the Lord. [ ] tant it is to listen, to follow, and to obey the voice of the Holy Spirit in the Christian walk. I highly recommend the read."

Judy LaRose, President of Spring Hill Aglow International, Florida

"Jacque Coffee has penned a Spirit-filled treasure chest of prophetic insight concerning the challenging times in which we live. She has 'cut to the chase' with a scripturally-backed no nonsense approach to our rapidly changing world. This book will help inspire faith and strength for battle-weary believers struggling with the uncertainties of today. Well done Jacque."

Pastors Chuck and Joan Poole, The House of Grace Covenant Church

"Pastor Jacque Coffee is an anointed and prophetic woman of God. She has a love for God, His Kingdom, and for the Body of Christ to awaken. She gives affirmation that the Church must become supernaturally alive and that ". . . we must take the opportunity to pour out to others" before it is too late! Her Spirit-filled writing as well as her teachings have enlightened, touched, and won many hearts."

Pastor Rachael Von Nostrand, House Of Faith, Inc.

This Practical Powerful Prophetic: 40 Days to Hearing God's 24/7 Voice is the raw Truth staring you square in the face. It will humble you and have you on your face before God. Embrace it!

Elaine Shelton, Greensboro, NC

WHAT OTHERS ARE SAYING ABOUT THIS BOOK

"Absolutely Awesome. You are putting into written form answers to questions many people have been asking. They are searching because their confidence level has been damaged along the way and they are not quite sure if they are hearing God or not. You have given wonderful illustrations to help us GET IT!"

Pastor Pat Pickens, House Of Faith, Inc.

"Jacque Coffee writes in an extraordinary way. This book will inspire, equip, and most importantly, *help us realize that EVERYTHING is prophetic.* God is always speaking, but we are not always listening."

Pastor Marion Esposito

"Beginning in her 20s, Jacque accepted the difficult discipline of daily prayer and confession, study, silent reflection, and invocation of the Divine through journaling. I sense the power of God flowing in her obedience to take on the enormous task of writing a book for God's kingdom people: these words will strengthen EVERY READER. My spirit is thrumming from Jacque's powerful words of scripture, her mature, wise and discerning gifts of commentary, and her challenge to live in the presence of the Holy 24/7!"

Linda B. Selleck, author of *Gentle Invaders: Quaker Women Educators and Racial Issues During the Civil War and Reconstruction*

"Jacque's is the call to a super-natural and intimate relationship with God—one that affects life 24/7. *This Practical Powerful Prophetic* awakens and inspires the believer toward relationship with the Living God who loves without restraint, feels with empathy, and gives without strings. With her understanding of the value of personal experiences, dreams, and visions exchanging between us and our God, this book is about the relationship that makes the difference in 'super-neutral' or supernatural in the believer's life."

Dr. James R. Pickens, House Of Faith, Inc.

"You haven't had a 'wake up call' like this Coffee produces. Jacque Coffee's prophetic vision rattles the keys to the Kingdom and encourages believers to unlock as many Kingdom doors as possible before our Lord's return!"

Jerry B. Byrd, Jr., beneficiary of Grace

"God had been speaking into Jacque's life to write this book. Then she received a prophetic word that everything that was supposed to go into this book had already been placed in her heart and it was time to move on it. I was blessed to be part of that process and read a chapter, pre-release. *This Practical, Powerful Prophetic* provides insight to hearing the prophetic word of God for your practical today life-style and shows you how to live it without compromising. For those who have trouble interpreting King James English this will make it understandable, a truly inspirational book."

Pastor Mark Long, Ms. Div., Home and Global Outreach

"*This Practical Powerful Prophetic: 40 Days to Hearing God's 24/7 Voice* brings fresh revelation that shatters the world's noise, silences the distractions, and awakens our senses to the voice of the One who loves us so passionately. Pastor Jacque Coffee captures the essence of how God pursues us in His amazing ways. We can learn to listen—to hear, feel, taste and see that practical, powerful prophetic voice of God."

Pastor Mark Howell, House of Faith, Inc.

"All I can say is—that was fantastic! Jacque takes a pragmatic approach to a not so pragmatic subject and turns it into a relevant guide for helping us tune into the things of God, the prophetic. A wake-up call to the church, to all (Eph. 5:14)."

Pastor Kelli Howell, House Of Faith, Inc.

THIS PRACTICAL POWERFUL PROPHETIC

THIS
PRACTICAL
POWERFUL
PROPHETIC

40 DAYS TO
HEARING GOD'S
24/7 VOICE

JACQUE COFFEE

JUMPING
CANVAS
PRESS

Spring Hill, Florida

Published by Jumping Canvas Press
Spring Hill, Florida

Cover and Interior Design by Imagine! Studios
www.ArtsImagine.com

Front Cover Images: Michal Bednarek/Bigstock.com & scenery1/Bigstock.com

ISBN: 978-0-9846675-3-6
Library of Congress Control Number: 2015918130

First Jumping Canvas Press printing: November 2015

"All things were made by Him, and without Him was not anything made that was made. In Him was the life; and the life was the light of men."

JOHN 1:3-4

This is your season to see and hear Holy Spirit's Words to you —

Jacque C. Orlando

"But when he, the Spirit of truth, comes, he will guide you into all the truth. He will not speak on his own; he will speak only what he hears, and he will tell you what is yet to come. He will glorify me because it is from me that he will receive what he will make known to you."

JESUS (JOHN 16:13-14)

Practical. *Adj.* fitted for action or useful activities.

Powerful. *Adj.* Potent, effective; having great power, authority, or influence; mighty.

Prophetic. *Adj.* Of or pertaining to what God has said; of divine inspiration. What is declared by either a God-inspired prophet, or through different means, *i.e.* dreams, visions, and pronouncements.

This. *Pronoun* Used to indicate a (noun) as present, *nearer in time or place,* or by way of *emphasis*:

"*This* practical, powerful prophetic is *your* heritage in Christ. Here. Now."

TABLE OF CONTENTS

ACKNOWLEDGMENTS

WITH GRATEFUL APPRECIATION TO . . .

. . . my 94-year-old father, Francis (Frank) Orlando, whose worldview has had its base in all things logical, practical, and well-reasoned. A *base*, as he explains, is "a chemical compound that *reacts* with an *acid* to form a *salt*." It sure does. I'm not sure which one either of us has been to each other, but our base of communication often yields salt and light in my world. Dad, thank you for sharing the wisdom in your memory bank with me; I'm glad we're both here for this season.

. . . all my children, family, and clan. I love you.

. . . my Apostle, my Pastors, friends and prophets who encouraged me to bring forth this message in this season. Thank you.

. . . You, Father, who made all things. It thrills me that You are speaking 24/7, opening our ears and eyes for an open heaven: Your Kingdom, come.

TODAY'S NEW(S)

"First things first. Your business is life, not death. And life is urgent: Announce God's Kingdom!" (Luke 9:60)

The mandate Jesus urgently declared, that we should announce God's Kingdom, came a long time ago. Is it old business today, or the message of the hour? You'll choose for yourself in the next forty days as we learn how to hear God's 24/7 Voice. This kingdom is one of ruling and reigning with Christ; of behaving as holy agents and ambassadors of the King; having and commanding His authority in His Spirit; of living and declaring as Ambassadors what will happen because of this King Jesus. These actions are highly charged with the prophetic. They are not charged with religion and rules. These are the days He is revealing the prophetic atmosphere of all things Kingdom oriented because the time is short and He will be returning soon.

But wait. Didn't Jesus say "the Kingdom of God is within you?" (Luke 17:21) *Who* was He saying that to? And when? "To you have been given the secrets of the Kingdom" (Matt. 13:11): who was He saying *that* to? I believe it's like this: In this season, the people of God who have heard the voice of God in Jesus Christ are to walk and exercise the prophetic fulfillment of the Words of this Kingdom because it is now inside us by His Word: a prophetic fulfillment about to happen whenever He says.

The personal scheduled re-entry of Jesus Christ as LORD is near and an electrical charge is in the air. It resonates in that place in our hearts where His Word has taken hold. Expectancy and Resistance. Heat and Coldness. God and His glory. **The Word is *happening.***

Prophetic passages inscribed in all of the Old and New Testaments are coming to pass, closer and faster than ever before

Worship has taken on a new tone, one of expectation that causes our own hearts to demand we "change our own tune" to the sounds of heaven

And yes, the world *is* heating up: the enemy is furiously at work because his time is short

I believe that this very day the world sits on the very edge of the changing of the guard into the antichrist's "one world," and the ful-fillment of the remaining prophetic events-to-come "in the last days" written thousands of years ago. At the same time **I am certain the kingdoms of this world are soon to become the Kingdom of our God!** (Rev. 11:15) We, as wholehearted adopted sons and daughters through relationship with Jesus Christ as Lord are preparing to be part of the greatest outpouring of the Holy Spirit in the world, ever. The shift is changing the landscape of hearts, nations, and lands, and will culminate with the ushering in of the Kingdom. These perspec-tives are braided together in this book.

Can you feel it? The Church is being prepared. *This Practical Pow-erful Prophetic* is a unique expression of God's 24/7 Voice regarding His "next moves." You'll want what He has in here.

A DEVOTIONAL. A WAKE-UP CALL. A MANIFESTO.

INTRODUCTION

This Practical Powerful Prophetic is to activate this generation to live wholeheartedly (*Gung-Ho!*) in God's prophetic Holy Spirit by recognizing and responding to His 24/7 Voice. For such a time as this.

We are the Body of Christ: the most precious group of journey making, risk taking, glory preaching, gap-breaching kings and priests the world has ever seen. **And most of us don't even know *that is who we are.*** Yet. This book is for *your* season of change . . . of perspective. From earthly to heavenly.

We all thrive with a spiritual awakening and activation for our ears and eyes, hearts, hopes, and end-time action. Even the *format* of this book will help unite Kingdom themes in our hearts; but the *content* is full, rich, and explicitly written for you to interact with. That's because it is **your life in God's life** we are talking about in *This Practical Powerful Prophetic.* The terms and headings below will be used throughout.

- **A devotional.** Each day we'll come to a feasting table where the Word of God openly reveals who you are meant to be: who the real *you* actually is! Like a priest, devote *yourself,* pray for *yourself* and others, and believe God. Worship like a king. *Prophesy to yourself,* by hearing His 24/7 Voice. This is a strong stand, but it's the New Covenant one Jesus *showed us to take* in all His ministry.

- **A wake-up call.** Today is the day to turn it all over to God and turn on the light of a new day. Where you've been sleeping or sloppy with your walk in Christ, or just plain AWOL, God's mercy abounds to *us if we turn to Him* with all our hearts. Every day that goes by there is a battle for your soul. Every day we don't exercise our place in Christ, the enemy gets more comfortable. Do it today because tomorrow you'll already need to be there. I am not exaggerating.

- **A manifesto.** The *prophetic charge* of the Holy Spirit *is* your call. It defines your Christian walk in the Kingdom. We wonder what we can do of significance, when *who we are and the Kingdom we announce* is the call of Jesus. This becomes your personal manifesto. Here is the fountainhead of your significance.

Chapter titles. These are deliberately meant to take you to the right side of your brain, where the creative, intuitive, and free-form holds sway. This part of our mind is particularly open to spiritual life matters. We need this prophetic hearing from our prophetic Lord. When blended with the left side of the brain's workings: logic, analysis and practicality, we begin to get a glimpse of the *God who is all these things* and so much more. Being led by Holy Spirit requires this interaction: it's our "whole mind."

Scriptures and Verses are identified in parentheses (so you will go back and read them for more depth without stopping the flow of the thought). Your Bible(s) should be with you for this 40 Days. If you don't go back and reach into the Spirit and the Word, you'll miss the purpose for any 40 Days to Anything. Reading the verses, and the content around them, takes you into deeper understanding with the likelihood that you'll become immersed and your whole nature will be changed.

One chapter per day. Each "chapter" is called a **Day:** "On *this* Day you are opening a new Chapter in your life." This is like *every day* should be. Knowing this will carry you further than forty days, further into your future, into "the season of *your* supernatural" fulfillment in Jesus.

The subtitle. "40 Days to Hearing God's 24/7 Voice" is best entered as a 40 day *fast,* hence the number of chapters. The number forty in the Bible usually includes a story of testing and trial that leads into a new season of maturity, power and favor when entered with humility, obedience and faith developed over that long season. Maybe a "40 days (or years) to anything" in Christ is more of an Isaiah 58 type of fast: a lifetime of lifestyle. For me, it's been a 40 Day Slow. Forty years ago, I thought I would be Moses by Monday. Today I am surprised God wants to use me at all at this point. Forty years ago I thought the plan was easy: just *do* it. I was reading my tennis shoes by mistake. I *assumed* (uh-oh) I understood the good plan of God because I read it and understood the words logically: "Oh, I get it! Okay God, now let's go!" And go, we did, into forty years in the desert and around the mountain. Happily, nothing goes to waste in God's economy, and everything counts in His Kingdom activity. The vision will come in its time. It just takes a while for God to put things into place. That season, I believe, is here for you. This is the season of your supernatural story with God.

A 24/7 Voice. Yes, you have "homework" at the end of each daily entry. It's about internalizing and personalizing your experience in a creative active way. When you've stumbled on revelation, enter it. This is to help you ground your stand. If you write it down and go away, even far away: you can come back and pray, and God will pick up with you where you left off, though I advise against assuming this is the acceptable way to walk with God. Remember the words, **40** days, *forty* **years.**

That's why you want perpetually **open ears,**
open eyes . . . for an open heaven

Manifesto. At the end of each Day's insights you'll find an affirmation called, a *Manifest*. Demonstratively take every revelation you get from God as yours in the Name above all names. Commit it to God to complete in you, and *declare* God will do it in you without your resistance because The King of kings is your Daddy! When you discover your heritage, take it to heart, and make it *your* manifesto, even the testimony of Jesus.

Appendices and other helps.

1. Get familiar with many helps in each Appendix at the end of the book

2. Use your Concordance along with your Bible
3. Take notes that Holy Spirit can form into revelation
4. Read, go online and research, have conversations, and practice forming responses
5. Get in a full-Gospel, Word-believing, Holy Spirit-Baptized, complete-Bible-loving church today
6. "... kindle afresh the gift of God which is in you ..." (2 Tim. 1:6)
7. Settle it at every stage in your heart to go *Gung-Ho!*

Journal. Buy one and use it every day. Personalize it: add color, art, quotes, and whatever "speaks to you." But most important, bring everything prayerfully and intentionally to the table as you embrace this practical powerful prophetic. Do your part to make sure what you see, hear, write, and say are true according to the Word. Getting creative usually brings up questions. That's great, because God has answers.

When God Speaks: Every so often as you read, you'll see a font change to a particular group of sentences. It is to identify these portions as prophetic interchanges with the Lord. You will be reading many such interchanges because they have literally transformed lives. Here is an example of God speaking into our time and space frame:

> "You weren't dreaming when I put that lively hope in you. This is the season to walk in it. Though it was delayed, yet it still comes: it's the perfect time in My plans for you. This is the reality of *the Kingdom of God coming close* that you hear all around you. Good news once again in a dry and thirsty land! Yes, you hear the sounds of war, the sounds of groaning. You hear the sounds of birth pangs, of the Spirit blowing in winds of My change. I am bringing to *fruition!*
>
> And I Am offering you a fire in *your* belly. It will consume you with the greatest joy and strength you have ever experienced when I show you what I have planned all along! So let's work together to fulfill those things that remain to be fulfilled. And one of those things is *you.*"
>
> *It is a Kingdom moment when you realize*
> *you're part of God's Royal Family*

PROLOGUE

WHAT IS "PROPHETIC"?

*"And I fell at his feet to worship him. And he said unto
me, See thou do it not: I am thy fellowservant, and of thy
brethren that have the testimony of Jesus: worship God: for the
testimony of Jesus is the spirit of prophecy." (Rev. 19:10)*

New Testament prophecy and the creative and personally prophetic ways God speaks (like He revealed in dreams to Joseph, angelic appearance to Mary, and hundreds of other biblical examples) are what we are going to zero in on in learning His 24/7 voice, but the words of the Old Testament prophets are welcome. I don't know if Perry Stone was the originator of this comment, but it aptly describes the connection in both sides of The Book: "The Old Testament is the New Testament *concealed*; the New Testament is the Old Testament *revealed*." If God's ways are His words, and are practical and powerful enough to have created the universe, speak promises that have waited thousands of years and still come to pass, and bring forth God's Deliverance and Salvation in Jesus the Christ, **then we need to hear clearly and see accurately, not just the facts, but the atmosphere of heaven they live in.** How important is that?

*The prophetic nature of God, of Christ-in-us, is the
spiritual counterpart to the air we breathe*

This atmosphere of heaven produces prophetic action. But like describing air, describing a *prophetic atmosphere* requires us to describe what lives in it, what actions can come of living in it. The invitation in this book is easy: seek and find, knock and it'll open, ask and it shall be given to you. Does that sound familiar? To put down roots for this definition, let's read this prophetically defining passage. Then we can answer a few questions.

> "And when he was come nigh, even now at the descent of the mount of Olives, the whole multitude of the disciples began to rejoice and praise God with a loud voice for **all the mighty works that they had seen**; Saying, Blessed *be* the King that cometh in the name of the Lord: peace in heaven, and glory in the highest. And some of the Pharisees from among the multitude said unto him, Master, rebuke thy disciples. And he answered and said unto them, I tell you that, if these should hold their peace, **the stones would immediately cry out.** And when he was come near, he beheld the city, and wept over it, Saying, **If thou hadst known, even thou, at least in this thy day, the things which belong unto thy peace! But now they are hid from thine eyes.**" (Luke 19:37–42 emphasis mine)

1. "All the mighty acts that they had *seen*" . . . many saw mighty acts but *saw nothing* that would convince them that Jesus was the Messiah. How did that happen? When God's voice spoke of Jesus as being His beloved Son in whom He was well pleased, *they* heard thunder, that's all. (Matt. 3:17) Their spiritual seeing and hearing was shut down because they lived spiritually *asleep*, in a fear-inducing religious culture. They dismissed and dishonored Him, so they literally stopped the flow of the things of God.

2. "The stones would cry out?" Really? Was He simply using a figure of speech? If we were prone to worship the creation more than the Creator, we would say, sure, stones can cry out and "sing," because they have a unique vibration and energy field. The scientific field of Physics tends to agree on a molecular level, but most scientists don't want to go further with faith. New Agers would agree, but they would not agree that Jesus who made them is to be worshiped as King of kings and Lord of lords. And as Christians? Jesus said stones cry out. I think I have missed something. There's a need for my prophetic ears to open to hear the sounds of the heavenly.

3. "If they had known" (or, understood when they saw and heard) what they were seeing, their peace would have been great. Inner peace, peace in their country, peace for their progeny: how many ways could the things that belong to their peace have been theirs, had they listened with their hearts! But because they were hardened in their eyes, ears and hearts, the very things they wanted were hidden from their eyes. Even Nicodemus had a difficult time bridging the gap, and *he wanted* to know.

All of nature is *created* substance: "All things were made by him; and without him was not anything made that was made." (John 1:3) All of creation speaks of Him . . . *and apparently to Him.* As the crown of creation you would think we would hear these messages all the time. Doesn't it sound suspicious to you? Like there is a lot more we can hear from God on a daily level?

> *The gifts of the supernatural, including the prophetic, are essential for the discovery of God as our force of faith*

If all we can say about these things is that Jesus was talking figuratively, how will we interpret these words: "All the fullness of the Godhead is found bodily in Jesus Christ" (Col. 2:9). If you aren't thinking supernaturally, you could never believe for a minute that God's fullness is in us through Jesus Christ! What a prophetic statement in a letter to the Colossians!

HEARING GOD'S 24/7 VOICE

We will discover in this forty days, **7 Aspects of "The Testimony of Jesus"**

1. God's Spirit pulls back the veil and **reveals** the "Living Word"

2. God's Spirit **opens** our ears to the sounds of glory in His universal language

3. We **individually** see God's Word, in Christ, applying to *everything*: events, objects, interactions, time, seasons, yesterday, today, and tomorrow

4. He speaks inspired-by-God **object "lessons"** that describe who He is to us to set us free

5. We **receive** God's wisdom through *unseen* **things**: dreams, visions, words of knowledge, wisdom

6. His Spirit *explains* **mysteries** in our ears as we seek Him

7. God **enlarges** our borders and **understanding** of the Truth

The Pharisees could have changed the course of their history and human history by seeing and hearing accurately. The Truth. But they knew only the restriction and controlling power of the Law. They thought God was one thing and when Jesus showed Him to be "other" than that, without real relationship with the Father, they froze. They missed it. They missed the day of their visitation. Their eyes remained closed. Blind. We can take a lesson from them. **And that would become prophetic in our lives.**

God's 24/7 Voice is His Word in a multitude of voices. Yours should be one of them. Today, let's begin to move deeper in the Practical Power of The Supernatural supply of God. This life in the Spirit makes all of life a new season of expectation. Starting on Day One. A 24/7 Voice. One day at a time. Is your journal close by?

PART 1
GROUNDED STAND

PRACTICAL AND PROPHETIC

"What other nation is so great as to have their gods near them the way the LORD our God is near us whenever we pray to him?"

DEUTERONOMY 4:7

DAY 1
KINGDOM ATMOSPHERE

God's Kingdom Atmosphere is breaking into this earth in these days to awaken His Church and the world to what's coming. HE is returning, this time, in great glory and power. We are to be with Him. Are you with me? So let's begin with how He rules in this contest. He is practical, but He works prophetically.

First to be practical, let's understand how He is. He is holy. God's Kingdom Atmosphere is worlds away from how we live our lives **in the flesh**. That's point one. Point two is similar: here in western cultures, we've been taught that receiving knowledge comes as someone pours it into our heads, with hardly a thought process needed: just eat it and go, regurgitate and repeat as needed. There's no need for reflection, rumination, or consideration. We think we become "smarter" by sheer volume of input. Books, talks, class work, testing all have taken on this tone of "pour-in" over decades of instruction. It's mostly information passed into our left brain where we categorize and label, thinking we have "lived it." Isn't this about as *impractical* as we can get? The atmosphere here smells of man's works and accomplishments.

> *Here is practical: we want His supernatural download of faith so we can live as we were designed to live in Him*

A dry, predictable, dictated religious faith is not His teaching method. But a practical, powerful prophetic one is. He has a supernatural perspective on life here on earth for every son and daughter of God. This is God's intention on our behalf. The prophetic is a joy-filled expectancy and discovery that God is:

- revealing His will for the long haul, till it is complete
- making visible His immediate intention to eyes that see

- inviting us into something we're personally to respond to or with
- providing in-sight, reality, and applicability to the already established Word of God

How does all this happen? It practically happens as we realize that everything coming our way is *prophetic* because God is for us! He is involved even when we aren't. But so much better is being involved with Him. We first change our thinking to His ways of thinking. "The prophetic" is not the acts or the objects: it is the Kingdom atmosphere in which acts happen and in which God uses objects to alert us. These are the things we're going to explore here in this book.

> *"Then he answered and spake unto me, saying, This is the word of the LORD unto Zerubbabel, saying, Not by might, nor by power, but by my spirit, saith the LORD of hosts." (Zech. 4:6)*

When God speaks, when the prophets spoke, when supernatural and natural events happened that have been chronicled in those biblical pages, *they are prophetic in nature because God is in them by His Spirit.* They were working to will and to do of His good pleasure. (Phil. 2:13) The Lord created the human in His own image, a spiritual being, so His Spirit could make Himself at home there the moment we invite Him as our treasured guest. We just have to be willing, available, and obedient. *Easy*, right? Yes, I'm laughing, too.

Hearing personally from Holy Spirit opens our ears and eyes to a reality of His Word that changes us in ways head knowledge can't. The living Word, Christ Jesus Himself, becomes perpetually and prophetically in-progress toward fulfillment:

- He fulfils our deepest longings for closeness, value, meaning and love
- He affirms inside us that God is alive and true, and *for* us
- He prepares us for everything so we are ready and without fear
- He awakens us to the revelation nature of His life
- He shows us things to come

Blessings like these, and many more, are not so much incidents, accomplishments or benefits so much as **they are the very spirit in which we live**. Can you see the fuller measure in "seeing" this way? They are part of the spiritual culture that shows us who and how God is, and who we are in Him. And those are the two steps of faith that make a walk, *practical* and *prophetic*.

My Kingdom atmosphere will ignite the world with Holy Spirit fervor, signs and wonders. When I AM (is) in your midst, it's a new Pentecost. It's a new season, not like anything you ever managed to accomplish, and better than you ever dreamed. People historically make monuments and missions, but when My Kingdom comes in your heart, the overwhelming description of it is not work, but LIFE; not *force* but **fulfillment**! Breathe in. As surely as I have breath says the Lord, I will perfect that which concerns you. Breathe afresh, breathe in My Kingdom atmosphere as it comes closer and closer and closer! For you have a lively hope and a powerful future in Me.

The faith of the Body of Christ is centered in an active, holy, on-fire relationship: we will see and we will hear, and heaven will open.

A 24/7 VOICE

Welcome to your first journal entry. Look up Ephesians 1:7, 8. Journal to the Lord: "I want to see You, Jesus. What do You look like?" Zoom in to see His *heart attributes. Ask Him why* you chose the heart attributes you named, seeing as there are so many you might have named. He will have a response that might reveal something you need to know about yourself. He's all about freedom.

MANIFEST

"God, I'm ready and desperate for your Kingdom Atmosphere. I will see and hear Your ways and Word; Your world. I may have lived like I was starving myself before now, but I'm tired of living a half-awake, half-baked life. You said I can know it: I want to know Your Kingdom, Your power and Your glory, right here in my heart."

WALKING IN HOLY PLACES

Just showing up at church on Sunday for your spiritual "fix" for one hour or till noon's feeding time (if your Saturday night wasn't too grueling) is no 24/7 walk. It's in the context of western culture that Christianity has gotten so soft-serve and chilly.

But if you go to Africa, church begins when it begins and goes on for the day and into the night, and maybe for days after that. Why is that? I'll tell you why! Because when you finally get there you have traveled on foot with your children, your tent, your kitchen appliances, food and animals for three days. *That* kind of sacrifice deepens fellowship with the body of Christ. *That* kind of devotion generates an attitude of willing and hungry expectation for God to show up. *That* heading out of the "comforts of home" to meet with God severs ties with the world you literally walked away from. *That* is what hearing a 24/7 Voice "looks like." *That* is what you call a breeding ground for miracles and wonders. And *that* is a good thing: they need them. And we need *that*.

And so it is, that it's at this time in the season of earth time that you're going to hear the voice of the Spirit calling you to get this deepest part of you in order: your priorities. This season is a time when you *must* hear God's 24/7 Voice: it's not extra or extraneous. It's not optional. And it's nothing new. It was this way in the early church when the fires of persecution were raging to reduce them to cinders.

We know what happened. *Just the opposite,* the church grew stronger and more beautiful. The 24/7 Voice of the Overcoming Church still praises God today and proclaims the victory in Christ Jesus. Can you hear them? Seek them out; find them, learn from them, and be built up.

Let's visit a people who *really* needed to hear and *really* needed their priorities rearranged. It was to people in Corinth, Greece, that God sent Paul. They lived in one of the most heathen cities in the Middle East in its time. They were among the most carnal Christians Paul had ministered to. They quibbled over non-essentials; they played favorites; they even turned their heads to sexual sins our own generation still blushes at (and that's not easy to do). They lived in a culture so steeped in spiritual pollution that when it seeped into the church, it yielded some of the filthiest behavior *un*imaginable.

It is to these people God had Paul go to and then write to with some of the most powerful provisions ever recorded!

> *"However, we speak wisdom among those who are mature, yet not the wisdom of this age, nor of the rulers of this age, who are coming to nothing. But we speak the wisdom of God in a mystery, the hidden wisdom which God ordained before the ages for our glory, which none of the rulers of this age knew; for had they known, they would not have crucified the Lord of glory. But as it is written: "Eye has not seen, nor ear heard, nor have entered into the heart of man the things which God has prepared for those who love Him.*

> *"But God has revealed them to us through His Spirit. For the Spirit searches all things, yes, the deep things of God. For what man knows the things of a man except the spirit of the man which is in him? Even so no one knows the things of God except the Spirit of God. Now we have received, not the spirit of the world, but the Spirit who is from God, that we might know the things that have been freely given to us by God.*

> *"These things we also speak, not in words which man's wisdom teaches, but which the Holy Spirit teaches, comparing spiritual things with spiritual. But the natural man does not receive the things of the Spirit of God, for they are foolishness to him; nor can he know them, because they are spiritually discerned. But he who is spiritual judges all things, yet he himself is rightly judged by no one. For 'who has known the mind of the LORD that he may instruct Him?' But we have the mind of Christ" (1 Cor. 2:6–16).*

You will never be His hardest case, and neither will I. Holy Spirit is committed to help us "see" with spiritual eyes; help us "hear" from Him. Deep things: *for you!* Mysteries and hidden wisdom: for *you!* That's what Paul the Apostle just described to a group I might have labeled as *hopeless*, except that I was one of them.

A prophetic word calls us: "Be immersed!" Hearing in our hearts, we are raised again to new life. Prophetic words have the power to call these things into being

Walk with me a few more steps into holy places. The word we know as, *baptize,* comes from the Greek word, *baptiso.* I was baptized into Christ. I was then baptized in the Holy Spirit. *Baptiso* was not even originally a "spiritual word," but a simple explanation for a process that happens organically:

- If you have cucumbers and stick them in a salty brine, they become pickled. They will never again taste like cucumbers. They have been immersed until their substance has been changed forever. They done-been *baptiso*ed
- Likewise, a wood boat floats until it goes down into the deep and becomes saturated with water: then it'll never again be fit for floating because its organic chemistry has changed. The wood is waterlogged and can eventually become like rock because its nature has been irrevocably transformed by the immersion process

So it is with you if the Spirit of God initially came to you and you are still abiding in Him, and He in you, in deeper and growing power. *So it is with you* if you still, and today, hunger and thirst after righteousness. *So are you* if you don't faint in the evil day. *So are you* if you seek God with all your heart. *So are you* when you love Him with all your heart, soul, strength and life. *So are you,* when you ask for the Holy Spirit and then jump in, and then never climb out but cling to Him to take you deeper.

This is prophetic promise for you! These are not simply words from a page! You need to grab them by faith, the prophetic gesture that generates fulfillment in earth-time. This practical powerful prophetic is the atmosphere of the Kingdom of God in us: it is a holy place that calls us to a wonder-full life.

*His nature, and our **state of being,** calls for us to*
sit with Him in heavenly places today

When we walk in holy places, you'll never imagine how many different places that is! The idea of living immersed in the Spirit of God became exciting in this vision one morning.

I saw cars in a violent storm on a rain-clogged street as they were coming to an intersection. They had to stop. I thought they had stopped for a red light but it was because there was a flooding problem. It was a problem with flooding, alright. I saw a very deep river right at the intersection; and in that water I saw men and women bobbing up and down, heads and shoulders visible, while they faced the people in the cars! The water was apparently well over their heads, but they seemed to be in no danger of drowning. I also saw that they were placed right there for that very moment of interaction at the intersection.

I asked the Lord, what am I seeing? His answer: "The coming floods of both trouble and triumph are here. You are seeing the latter rains before the harvest pouring in. Those conveyances are stopped by the force of the same river in which the saints are thriving with hearts ignited! The people in the cars are perplexed and astounded because this intersection is earth meeting the heavens-opened-up. They sit, their own strength (conveyance or vehicles) stopped, wondering what to do. The people of God in the waters see their trouble: they need to intersect with God! So they face them, bobbing up and down, shocking and arresting them with their boldness and confidence.

This is the authority that flowing in the Spirit of God carries with it: it starts things and stops things mightier than the person speaking it. It beckons all to come to the waters of life and rise above life. It shouts of life in the Holy Ghost and urges scared travelers caught in the storm to take joy and peace in believing. This is victory, that you can live immersed in the river of living waters!

Never fear, children, for I AM your transportation in any deep waters you will intersect with. You shall face them and arrest them, boldly, and with confidence."

If there is anything the alive and persecuted church throughout history, around the world, and in our own backyard would agree on, it would be that we need to *"hear* the word of the Lord." It's about a relationship with God that is not simply, the God who *filled* us with His Spirit thirty years ago, or the God that will one day do this or that. **It's about the God who is LORD now, in me, in this moment. He knows me and I know Him.** Today is where every life-changing moment happens. Now is when, and here is where, our "Great I *AM"* wants us to flow with Him. That is a holy place to walk, swim, and care enough to face off with the world. We can't "just show up" anymore in places like this. It becomes our home.

A 24/7 VOICE

Look up from your day and "see" around you. Listen for His voice to speak in your heart. Write it down. Go back to the *"So it is with you"* paragraph: slow down and listen. ***There is a stirring of hope and expectancy*** you need to respond to. Write it all out in your journal. Get used to this "writing it all out" part. Title it at the top of your page so you can find it later; there's a powerful **pouring** out God wants to do in you to **ignite** your heart.

MANIFEST

"Without You I could never walk in holy places: I wouldn't even have thought to! But You're making me wiser every moment I spend in Your presence. With the power of Your Holy Spirit in me, I walk with You through all moments and events of my life. And I do start, now."

DAY 3
FULLNESS OF TIMES

This book has been *forming* in me but *dormant* for forty years. Never underestimate a long formation period! That you are reading it now is the proof you need that the dreams God gave you early on are in His care till they suddenly spring forth. In the meantime, while we "wait" we live and change, we learn and get experience, experience begets hope, and we head into Romans 5 where the love of God is shed abroad in our hearts by the Holy Spirit which is given to us. (Rom. 5:1–5) Can you see that scripture is prophetic promise for us to profit from? Beyond our abilities, thinking and gifts, and above all troubles, adversities and set-backs, God promises He has a much bigger plan and picture for us.

Everywhere, in things large, in things inconsequential, yet used by God; in dreams, miracles, visions, and the opening of our eyes to see the times we live in, we absorb the heritage of God and the love He has for the Church. In the fullness of times, God brings forth what He has been working on: a masterpiece in you that you can't take credit for, so He gets the glory. Hearing God's 24/7 Voice dovetails with living holy and immersed in the Spirit, working unseen until it is seen.

The world around you is looking at your life to see if they can hear God's voice in you. They may not behave responsibly or live like you do; they may not like your faith; they may have other interests . . . but they are watching and listening. Just do something really inappropriate and you'll find out.

You won't see the difference in the world's ways and the
Spirit's ways until you see and hear prophetically

I'm sorry we have to go here. It won't take long because we all know where we come from. This is the reminder to never go back, as if you need one. We go here now to begin a prophetic reach with the testimony of Jesus, back to people still stuck there.

The whole world system apart from the Truth in Christ is held hostage in a counterfeit camp. It's nothing personal against anyone; it's just the default setting on humanity. Sin hurts people. They get hardened through the deceitfulness of the world, the flesh, and the devil (Heb. 3:13; Mark 4:15–17). Without submitting their hearts to God, they have to figure it all out themselves. It is *impossible* without the Living God in Christ Jesus. People don't ask for a message of freedom for one of two reasons. Either they are held captive to the spirit in them working to kill them (pride, lust, rebellion, hate, fear, unforgiveness, etc.), or, they are resistant until there is proof positive that "it" really works. They demand a "guaranteed or your money back" clause. They don't realize they *have* One: Jesus, raised from the dead; Jesus, ascended into heaven; Jesus, seated at the right hand of the Father God, ever living to make intercession for the saints. How will that message reach them if they refuse the Word in flat black and white form?

You are the message

Seeing *you* change and be transformed with a life and perspective you obviously never operated in before is convincing, and yes, prophetic. Maybe even unnerving and uncomfortable. When someone meets up with you after you've become a new creation in Christ, it could be the shock their eyes and ears needed. "My Lord, there must be a God; look who's come to Jesus!"

When I finally gave in to the invitation to belong to Him, I felt like my own salvation was **a prophetic biblical fulfillment.** What God started in me long ago by His own admission was now becoming reality as I came to know Jesus as Lord. "He sent His Word and healed me, and delivered me from my destructions." (Ps. 107:20) I zeroed in on this idea of prophetic fulfillments. I wanted to know what else belonged to us from the foundation of the earth. What I found and continue to find is that every word God speaks is prophetically designed to be accomplished in me as a human being, and *will be accomplished* from the Spirit to my life. (Is. 55:11)

It was the work on Calvary that regained mans' complete spiritual heritage lost by Adam. That prophetic fulfillment was the Great Turnaround for the entire creation, planned by God from before the foundations of the world, and carried out at the fullness of times by Jesus, the Son of the Living God.

As if *that* isn't prophetically charged enough, *we* have now been made the same righteousness of God in Christ Jesus! (1 Cor. 1:30; Rom. 3:22; Rom. 5:21) This is our Gospel, our good news. No wonder the enemy of God hates it and us, and tries to distort and disclaim it.

Please understand, the perversion of the supernatural by satan only proves that God's practical powerful prophetic existence is worth trying to copy. Satan's lies are a counterfeit, wherever they show up. But you shouldn't run from God's prophetic reality in Christ: that is an expression of His power to fulfill!

Many around you know *you* from *"before* Christ." In the fullness of times, when they hear and see the nature of God, the transforming love, this prophetic and miraculous attitude you flow in naturally, in the Name of Jesus Christ, and right before their eyes: **their gift of faith will come.** If not, you can't say you didn't offer it to them with your very life.

Look up and notice how things are being fulfilled. This is the season of the fullness of times. Where you once saw with natural eyes, you will see spiritual things happen that astound the world and turn hearts you thought could not turn. A visitation from God is "a strong invitation" to serve the All Mighty, and many you think would not bow to Me shall bow and hear My words when they see nature and events around them speak to them of Me. Everyone will be given the opportunity for their fullness of times to come forth, though not everyone will take it.

With your natural eyes you will see a tearing down of life and plans, but don't look with your natural eyes. That is what continually brought down the children of Israel. Gather what you have at hand, encourage your heart in the Lord, and in one accord begin to rebuild what has gone to waste. When the world sees My people building where tearing down has been the order of the day, many will open their ears and eyes. What they will see is My Spirit at work, not man's, doing what only GOD can do. Watch for it and see!

This is the **season** to prepare your hearts to hear and see miracles of nature, provision, and My plans coming to pass in the earth.

This is the hour to alert all you can, all who will hear My voice to be delivered.

Your part is **now**.

The Harvest is here.

A 24/7 VOICE

Outline your journal page in a wispy blue line of color. Blue is the color of the heavens and of waters. Both suggest an open and deep expanse. This now surrounds what you will be bringing to the surface. Describe a dream you have had that you have given up on. But do not leave it as "undone." Title your entry: "In the Fullness of Times." Write about three things:

1. About you. **Write down your hope**, and if applicable, what happened to kill it
2. **Find encouragement from His Word** that calls you higher, that suggests you believe again: but from this new perspective, that you consider it **spoken to you**.
3. **Then turn what you find into a declaration of intent from God** to turn things around

MANIFEST

"I am no longer simply, me; I am a new creation never seen before; a son of God in Christ. This is the season of Your fulfillments in me: I will testify with my life. Glory to Your Name."

DAY 4
WORDS WITH GOD

*"For the Lord GOD will help me; therefore shall I not be
confounded: therefore have I set my face like a flint, and
I know that I shall not be ashamed." (Isa. 50:7)*

The ultimate relationship is for God personally to live abundantly in us today in this life, where He opens our eyes to see and our ears to hear His 24/7 Voice. Anything less is not real life; anything more and we'll have to be in heaven.

In every Day's entry for forty days are spiritual connectors to what is prophetic. You will think about the words of each Day's title, you will reference the Word of God, and use examples of events, experience, words, visions, and dreams to activate a vision in you that starts to see ahead. You will become more watchful for divine inspiration for you personally. You'll probably head into some chapters and say, "Hey, I know about that! The Lord once told me. . ." These days of hearing God's 24/7 voice are showing you that in the everyday, even mundane hours, as well as the hours of stark raving calamity, He is speaking! Settle it in your mind right now: *He wants you to hear His voice.*

Words with God is not like "having (harsh) words with" someone, which means there has been a disagreement somewhere in the relationship. No, we get to hear from Him and interact with Him in unprecedented ways. If perchance we do disagree with Him, our relationship with Him should become so real that we understand in a moment that someone is wrong and He never is. I've shared with you already words He's spoken in my heart that have helped me change my mind. You'll read plenty more in the next thirty six days.

As I journaled late one night, I watched my words carefully as I put them on paper: I didn't want to be negative. So all that came out was a manufactured confession of trust. There was no life in it. It didn't touch my heart and I figure it didn't touch my Lord's. I was discouraged because of many sad and unfinished situations, and fighting off fears for the future. I knew it was "wrong thinking" so I expected a human type of response: *You shouldn't feel that way; that is wrong.* But My heart was quickened when He re-affirmed who He is in my life. The words were not mine, as I had been the one grousing for the last hour. But I had the pen, so I wrote it. You see, we are one . . . and so are we all in Him; and so this may be for you also.

"Don't be fooled and don't be alarmed. There is a fire in the presence of the Spirit of God, the likes of which you have not felt or imagined yet. You have cried out for this, hoped and waited, longing for the Presence of God in greater power. Don't think I haven't been preparing you through all this, through all your life. To every depth of need you have gone, My Spirit was there to walk with, warm you, and lighten your way. You came back, not because you figured it out, but by the power of My Spirit.

Look around you: Most of My people have gone through disappointment, great loss and discouragement. Many have backed off the Word and even walked away from Me, allowing their setbacks or seductions to overcome them. **Know this: I AM (is) not finished with them, and neither am I finished with you.** *Here's* **what you haven't figured into the mix yet: As surely as you've seen trouble, you can expect to experience your season of the supernatural**.

For I will have your attention in this troublesome time, and I will also attend you with power while I also contend with our enemy. He will raise all the hell he can in these last days, but **he cannot resist the standard I raise, for it is the very Kingdom of God installing itself in the earth.** For this is the season, and it is My own Word coming to fulfill all things, even everything I have told you already. Stay awake and aware, prepare your spirit and be ready also for the surprises I have for you. Start with this surprise: **you surely will *rejoice* in your day, regardless what happens *to* you and *around* you**. So says the Lord to His daughter."

The greatest awakening to God in the history of the world has already begun. Do you see what it is taking for it to come into being, much less into view? Trouble. That's where our world is today. As "nation rises against nation, and kingdom against kingdom," have you experienced the kingdom of darkness rising against the Kingdom of God? It's easy to see in the USA, as what had been established in righteousness is now being torn down in the name of many causes.

What God prophesies will happen: in the world,
to His enemies, and to and in you

Can I say that regardless what happens around us, His plans for us are ones of provision? Though lawlessness has increased in the name of progress, and lasciviousness in the name of love, it has all been prophesied. For the people of God who show the light of truth in the midst of darkness: come on, do you really think He will leave you or forsake you? If you're looking for a safe haven, it will be found in Christ alone. That, friends, is prophetic promise from His Word: set your face like flint and believe God no matter what comes. "Incline your ear, and come unto Me: hear, and your soul shall live; and I will make an everlasting covenant with you, even the sure mercies of David. Behold, I have given Him for a witness to the people, a leader and commander to the people." (Isa. 55:3, 4) Here is prophetic power waiting for you to take hold of right now. **Words with God are words with power.**

Before the Lord returns, history will repeat itself, evil will get worse and worse, and **the people of God shall be strong and do exploits**. God has sounded the alarm and His people are waking up and getting ready. Spiritual eyes are opening, and they are hearing their Lord say, let's finish this up and get on to glory! **These are the words with God that you will hear in your spirit**, undergirding you with new resolve and urging you to action. Start hearing them today! Say them to yourself. They are prophetic words which will be brought to pass in you if you will believe God to the exclusion of all other voices.

This **practical, powerful prophetic** is your heritage in Christ. Seeing it open up your world to a suddenly alive hope and fulfilling promises before He takes you home is nothing short of miraculous. That's what words with God will do. You can talk with Him any time, even 24/7. That's how He likes it. He can handle it. That's how He prefers it. Pretty neat that He loves you like that, right? This Day we begin to know Him better, hear Him deeper, and know He is love. If today you sense your need to be responsive to the Lord's return because "it's a lot sooner than when you first believed," respond today; **and welcome also your season of the supernatural.**

A 24/7 VOICE

John 5:20. If God were to speak to you, what would He say **today**? If it is to chastise you or condemn you, back up and remember that *He is for you* or He wouldn't have died for you. Today, knowing your own needs as you do, **how would He speak to you**? You can begin by telling Him the need, then *allow Him to speak back*. You aren't making up the words, but rather going back into your knowledge of who He is! Back into your relationship with Him. That should take the stress off you. You're listening, that's all. Listening is good, and worship opens the door to His voice. Your heart is the pen of a ready writer, as David said. You hold the pen, so when you hear, use it.

MANIFEST

"Ah, Lord God, I once had words with You only in arguments. From this day forward, I refuse to walk in rebellion, and demand my flesh to bow to Your ways and hear Your voice! You have always been all I needed, and today, I receive by faith the good promises You have waiting in this new season. I'm thankful You aren't finished with me."

DAY 5
IT'S TIME

I can't go further in this book without giving honor to the saints around the world who are in the furnaces of affliction. They are part of us, they are family. It has been noted that since 1900, more Christians have been martyred for their faith than all the other centuries since Christ rose from the dead, *combined*.

But wait, let's not go in that direction. Let's hear what the Spirit is saying because it is different from our heavy hearted sighs. After listening to a radio interview reporting that thousands of Muslims are coming to Jesus, the Messiah, here's what I heard:

> "There must be **a mighty powerful influence** at work, then, that is convincing millions of *God's enemies* to *convert to Christianity*. Believe it, I AM able. My death was as powerful on their behalf as on yours; they cannot kill My flesh and blood without knowing they have touched the Lord's anointed. The shedding of the blood of My people cries out and is a voice that will come back, not only in My ears but in *their* ears, night and day, day and night, **until I am able to have words with them**. Be brave and pray for this, a mighty deliverance."

Holy Spirit was making an aside to me, to turn fear into faith, as I ruminated on how the impossible happens! **The enemies of the cross come to the cross, too.** In spite of, even because of, the anti-Christ armies of ISIS and others, there is a mighty and supernatural salvation at work stronger than ever! Holy Spirit knows how to reach *every* heart! It's quite possible many people do really off-target things for all the wrong reasons, thinking they are doing it to please God. I might even know what that feels like.

His Word will continue to penetrate the darkness until it's time to take it out of the world. But I reckon He'll have to take us out first

It's Time. The Body of Christ is awakening, people are becoming part of Christ Jesus from every nation, from *every* people group, even the ones we cannot imagine becoming brethren in Yeshua, Jesus: murderers, idolaters, atheists, cannibals, and even democrats. The last outpouring of God is *pouring*! Prophetically speaking, it's the Latter Rain before the Great Harvest. When I say, it's time, that's what I mean. This practical, powerful, prophetic voice of God is telling us every day this "good news from a far country."

God-who-loves- our-enemies is sending dreams and visions of Jesus, while His own persecuted people are reaching out to them! It's happening everywhere: in Africa, the Ukraine, China, all the Muslim countries, and yes, in the United States of America. Around the world, in every language and tongue, there is God's 24/7 Voice. You may not hear it much on evening TV because He is mostly edited *there*. Yet, He cannot be silenced and we cannot be marginalized. Jesus said a powerfully prophetic thing about His life that everyone around Him missed:

"No one can take my life from me. I sacrifice it voluntarily. For I have the authority to lay it down when I want to and also to take it up again. For this is what my Father has commanded." (John 10:18 NLT)

Listen elsewhere for *your* victory. Hear those new brethren in Iran say that when they come to Jesus they understand full well that it may be their last day on earth; they make their choice to serve Jesus in full knowledge and fullness of joy. Hear it in your spirit and be comforted. It's time to strengthen yourself in this way. The day is coming soon when you may have to live *that* committed. Start practicing today.

Believers in Africa say they refuse to go underground. The more oppressed they have been, the more they have grown in numbers, in passionate love, and a humble and mighty perseverance! It reminds the world of the children of Israel in bondage in Egypt: they just keep multiplying and flourishing. There is something about the trials of life becoming ignited with the nearness and power of Jesus in the midst of trouble! It makes believers who are willing to die for what they are willing to live for. And their enemies see it!

While our present social system and government thinks it is removing all vestige of Christianity, God is doing a new thing! He is replacing lukewarm Christianity with a new breed of believer who's ready for war. He and she have *been through enough fire with God* that they have made up their minds. They're saying, "Guess what! I want Jesus; that's all I want. I want all of Him and I want to share all of Him. People have to know, and I'm gonna let them hear my voice. I don't care what it takes. I don't care if it is illegal. I don't care how it impacts me. He *must* be lifted up: **it's time**."

We are a mighty army in the power of His love. We are a great cloud of witnesses still on earth. (Heb. 12:1) It's time. God's Spirit is moving to reveal all Truth, whatever you will need to survive and stand in Him; and *He often does it through more-than-natural means.* Our brethren in dangerous countries attest to that.

We are to admit every bit of this breaking, quaking and reawakening around the entire *world as evidence that the gospel is being preached* to every nation! What happens next? Persecution? Of course. (Matt. 24:14) All this shaking, breaking, and reawakening is no coincidence. It has been prophesied everywhere in the New and Old Testaments: prophecies thousands of years old *now showing* at a theatre near you. Hallelujah. And *then* what? "Then shall the end come." That's what this time is.

A 24/7 VOICE

Journal your thoughts of how you feel about your enemies. Paragraph 1: Who they are. Paragraph 2: Why you don't like them. Paragraph 3: What you can learn from them or *Why you need them* [Look, I'm just the messenger].

MANIFEST

"LORD, Your plans and purposes have been under way for so long. Today is the day for You to reveal what's been concealed of the end of the matter! You will get me and mine ready! You go through everything, close with me, this I know, My keeper, my provider."

DAY 6
BEHIND THE "SEENS"

"So we don't look at the troubles we can see now; rather, we fix our gaze on things that cannot be seen. For the things we see now will soon be gone, but the things we cannot see will last forever." (2 Cor. 4:18)

When a stage play is being acted out, what we watch is out front on center stage. There, voices travel well and you get to see the details and nuances of all that's going on. But a lot is going on at the same time behind the scenes to impact what we see out front. Behind the painted scenery, lights, and curtains, stage hands are scurrying around with props, lights, ladders, and directing people here and there, all to make sure the play out front follows the plot. It's as fascinating to see back there as it is to watch out front.

There can hardly be a better analogy for what goes on behind every world arena, from people interactions to political agendas. When we know what's going on behind the scenes we understand it is a much bigger picture! The Bible explicitly tells us that behind the scenes we wrestle not with the flesh and blood we think is responsible for all our problems. (Eph. 6:12)

Sometimes our ability to distinguish between right and wrong, enemies and friends, safe and dangerous, good and evil, what is helpful and what is harmful . . . *is skewed.* Our accurate Spirit-filled vision can be clouded by pain, experience, opinion, bias, social pressure, flesh, constant repetition, intimidation, allure, the grandiose, fear, seduction, and many other seemingly random soul situations operating behind the scenes. What we need to *see* is the Truth. *Discernment* is seeing accurately the meaning and intention behind what is seen, said, intended and acted out.

The discernment factor is a vitally important interaction of the brain and the spirit, of our human spirit with God's Spirit. Discernment has to be built on The Truth or it is a false discernment; no discernment at all. If it becomes skewed, we are in trouble and don't know it. Look at how warped "truth" can become.

A Facebook post came around with a quote by Maximillian Robespierre, a leader of the French Revolution in the 1700s: "The secret of freedom lies in educating people, whereas the secret of tyranny is in keeping them ignorant."

Sounds good, right? I'm sure it passed onto many peoples' pages with no thought of there being a slight skew to it. Maybe they don't know Robespierre was instrumental in the French Revolution, the subsequent *Reign of Terror*, and the deaths of hundreds of thousands of people considered "enemies of the state." Knowing the person who posted it has a socialist, ultra-liberal worldview, I understood it a different way than he may have intended. Or maybe I didn't read it wrong at all. Here's what I mean. I re-posted and asked, What do you think? Did Robespierre leave out a small detail or two? Here's my take: "The Secret of Freedom Lies in educating people" . . . (my add) **in God's Truth**. "The secret of tyranny is in keeping them ignorant" . . . (my add) **through an education in lies and manipulative, destructive agenda.**

Adding these words specifically as *objective* qualifiers yields a potentially completely opposite meaning. What was a subjective comment by Robespierre (his thoughts, not God's objective truth) can hold many different agendas when seen in contrast to the way God thinks from His Word, which is truth. (John 17:17) Bringing this example to a conclusion, you see, some people think people are in bondage *because of* the Word of God! Holy Spirit discernment saves you from confusion and deception.

Remember, we are talking about words. Words are prophetic by God's own admission, and will accomplish what they are sent for. (Prov. 13:2; 18:20, 21) Only words without human-agenda spin, under the leading of His Spirit, are pure words. If a new generation is not blessed to have the Word of God wisely and readily available, but is being taught by people who manipulate words to manipulate society, how can they be reached? Can you see in these comments that we are discussing *battle strategies in the heavenlies,* and not simply disagreements in worldview?

Discernment is like a knife

Discernment cuts through what's on stage and heads directly backstage. It sharpens perception, and opens our ability to detect and distinguish between lies and other dangerous traps. Proverbs 8 and 9 say discernment and good understanding are our Spirit-formed and led friends. We need to know at least five different things from *seeing behind the seens.*

We Need to Know . . .

1. that we are following God and not some cleverly worded fraud
2. if what we are interacting with is of God or of another spirit
3. what to do when what we are interacting with is from another spirit
4. what His Word *means* so we aren't trapped into getting offended by it or turned aside by something else
5. how to speak to and deal with the situation that has been discerned as other than what it presents to be

If only the problem weren't a *big* one. Discernment would be a great help *if only* our culture had not decided it is not polite to call something wrong. *If only* it were not extremist and intolerant to say a certain thing is not what you choose to live by. *If only* the laws had not been sabotaged away from God's Word. *If only* relativism were not such a beautiful thing to those who want to do what *they* want to do, believe how *they* want to believe, and respond as nastily as they please anyway. *If only* our schools were not allowed to brainwash our children to disbelieve in God but accept every other spiritually (corrupt) thing. With all that, where is our discernment to land?

I grew up in a decade where truth still held sway in American schools, so discernment between good and evil was foundational to us. I was even required to learn the Books of the Bible when I moved south in the 1960s. I was stunned. I didn't even know what "the Bible" was. Not so today. It's far worse. Laws and school books have been rewritten and many teachers have been, too. Now the Bible, especially as the location of Absolute Truth, is not welcome.

The world has been morphing over the years, and today the Bible is *forbidden* in many places, yes, in our country. Soon you will be an enemy of the State if you adhere to this Book of all books. It will be forbidden in public, with the intention to be forbidden *in your heart* by the State. How is that *possible*? When the time comes that it is an ultimatum, the answer to that will be, **only if you let it!** America's Apostasy is hurtling it toward oblivion. **But it is not hurtling us into oblivion.** This is the hour God is preparing us for, in which He will be fulfilling many of His promises to, through, and in us.

Open ears . . . Open eyes . . . Open heaven

Behind the "seens" there is a world of spiritual activity. Angels war with demons. God's Word continues to advance. Heaven roars with praise. A great cloud of witnesses both in heaven *and* on earth, with loud voices, testify to the Truth. And the prophetic atmosphere of the Kingdom of God presses in on us behind the scenes, waiting for the moment to spring forth the return of our King, Jesus! Hallelujah.

In my Concordance, there are a number of words for discernment. A lot of them bear mentioning here because you'll see in a minute how connected they are with prophetic wisdom and perspective. I leave it to you to search these out for yourself. Discern:

- To understand and consider (Prov. 7:7)
- To cause to understand, to instruct (1 Kings 3:9)
- To know, to be acquainted with (Eccles. 8:5)
- To acknowledge (Gen. 27:23; 31:32; 38:25)
- To *see* (Mal. 3:18)
- To *hear* (2 Sam. 14:17)
- To examine closely, to judge or assess (1 Cor. 2:14)

Discernment is a matter of spiritual vision. According to my Thesaurus, discernment is an earmark of intelligence, it is the ability to see (perceive), and "make a difference."

If you hear, "*God is love*" from someone, *you* think, *Jesus died for my sins*. But someone else might hear, "that's why everyone in the world will go to heaven and there is no hell." That's a pretty big difference. Discernment is not the words we hear, but seeing through the words or actions to the intent of the speaker: his agenda, the spin, an ulterior motive or their worldview being expressed.

Today on Day 6 we are clearing a path to make a *difference* in our thinking and in how we relate to the world's input as it comes by. It's another step into the deeper and wider river of Truth. We access it through One Source: the Spirit of the Living God in Christ, Jesus, the Fountain-head of all Truth and Life.

Paul experienced many cultures and spirits that drove cultures in his day, not unlike we do. He knew the value of being trained by discernment, the importance of knowing what you are really dealing with: "But solid food is for full-grown men, for those *whose senses and mental faculties are trained by practice to discriminate and distinguish between what is morally good and noble and what is evil and contrary either to divine or human law.*" (Heb. 5:14 AMP) As the plot thickens, we'll be glad we laid hold on this "solid food" with prophetic promise: God's script will be played out in full, to a full house, and when the curtain comes down at the end of the age, we'll be left standing to give Him glory. A standing ovation, even behind the "seens."

A 24/7 VOICE

Draw a picture of a stage set with the stage and backstage. Make it look like a blueprint viewed from above, or like an actual perspective view. What will you have going on here on stage and what will be happening backstage? Make notations. For a stage hand to get from stage right to stage left, he has to have a pathway to get there that doesn't bring him out on stage or he will be seen out front. Think about that. What might that have in common with elements at work in our lives? Write, listen, find wisdom in His Word. You can add art, color, cut-outs, etc. if they inspire you.

MANIFEST

"I do not rely on my own wisdom, my own sight and discernment: Yours is perfect. I cling to Your help in this dangerous climate, with the promise that in Your hand is a way for me that is right, full and rich in You. You know me behind the scenes I make, and You still love me."

DAY 7
PAST, PRESENT, AND FUTURE

"What has happened before will happen again. What has been done before will be done again. There is nothing new in the whole world." (Eccles. 1:9 ISV)

What a prophetic verse! Some seasons do seem more prophetic than others. Many believers are discovering that the Feasts of Israel are some of those seasons. They are prophetic seasons, in that Jesus "just happened" to have been crucified on Passover, 2,000 years later. His return seems to be suggested in scripture as happening during the Fall feasts of ingathering. A lot is happening in these arenas because these are *God's* feasts we're talking about.

This is God bringing scripture alive in our own day, in your own life, able to impact nations and circumstances, for this season, when you thought it was over long before you came along. It's not about coming back under any law except for the law of Christ's love.

Then there is Christmas, which I grew up with and never knew the difference between Jesus and Santa Claus: why were they in the same story? Obviously my discernment hadn't become developed. I always loved the holiday: **there was something more there than met my eye.** Today, we still say, *'Tis the season'* around Christmas when Jesus still is "allowed to be born" in the manger every year. Even when I didn't know this was more than a children's story, His Spirit hovered over me all throughout the Christmas seasons of my youth. I can't help but associate the feeling I lived in at that time of year with how the disciples felt after Jesus had risen, *but they didn't realize it yet.*

Luke 24:13–32 relates that as the risen Lord Jesus came alongside several disciples walking along the road to Emmaus, the Presence of the Eternal One suddenly joined their eight mile journey. They were in such grief they didn't recognize Him. Just think, death had been swallowed up in life (1 Cor. 15:54), but there they walked, away from Jerusalem, full of sorrow and hopelessness, still blind to the presence of God. It can be that way with us if we aren't watchful. Jesus pressed in with the words from the Old Covenant that pertained to all that had happened. Past meets present. Their faith was now kindled. It felt like a burning inside, an unexplainable fire, and it was getting hotter.

Toward the end of the evening, when they all sat down to eat together, *and in the breaking of bread, He was recognized by them!* He had entered their space where they ate, drank and lived. Finally their eyes were opened! There at supper, they recalled the last supper they had shared with *Him.* Suddenly they saw their future! Their gut level feelings came out (which I should point out, were prophetically charged long before their minds knew) with the exclamation: *"Didn't our hearts burn within us* as we walked together and He opened up the scriptures to us?"

Right into your space is where the Spirit of God wants to live! Years ago, I experienced a beginning like this, a prophetic promise I would discover many years later in my future. Nothing could be finer than, after looking for Him, listening for Him, and reveling in a simple manger scene, I can look back and say, *Wow, my heart was burning within me before I ever knew Him to be who He is!* What in His Word have you read that sets your heart afire? Don't discard it as indigestion! It is prophetic promise to you.

You no doubt know friends and those closest to you who have excused themselves and headed in other directions because their hopes were deferred or they got offended. He's walked with *me* through very deep valleys. I have the distinct blessing to be able to say, against all odds, from which I thought I would never recover: I am now living the dreams and hopes God placed prophetically in my heart, long ago. Don't give up, *Give in* to His working on you so your future can be fulfilled as He desires.

I'm talking to people right now who are in Christ for many years. Friends have come and gone and not all exits were godly or blessed. Yet you clung to God and prayed and kept you heart pure as best you could; you blessed and didn't curse. There will be what people call, a "suddenly." The next thing you know you get a phone call. Restoration and forgiveness, tears and new beginnings. Holy Spirit mends hearts torn apart by the enemy; yes, healed in one hour. Past, present and future are changed in a moment. This is the beginning of the restoration of all things. About this season of God's supernatural, this is what He is bringing to pass:

"Are you ready to ride a wave of healing and provision with Me? There are dreams, hopes, prayers, and many things you've held onto for years, believing they were going to come through but didn't. Yet. They *are coming to fruition today.* Some things remain 'out there' waiting to be called into your space in the fullness of time. Know that this season is the meeting of past, present, and future *because of what time it is to Me.*

There is a great reward for the people of God whose faith has moved them over mountains against all odds, against the thief, against time and circumstance, against loss and grief. This is the season for My healing and favor to fit you into your time, into your space, the time and place you have held in your spirit for all these years. For the Lord has gone before you and made a place for you that you could never have produced.

And you thought I didn't remember! Children, **you shall yet again** put down roots and bear fruit upward, even as you saw in your spirit long ago. Now you are no longer children, but sons and daughters. Here is how to ride the wave of healing and provision: take your place in the waters, and as the wave of My Spirit rolls in, get up and *ride it now.* This is what it will feel like:

You'll have new hope where before, yours was done. You will grab hold of a strong determination to take every moment captive so you can be about our business together. A joyful insistence will rise in you to receive your heritage. Why not practice it today!

Look into My face and see how I love you, take courage in how present I AM! Hang out with Me and let us take our evening meals together. It's no longer about past tense, sorrows, *or* fear over future! I am setting you into **today's present tense** in order to make time your servant. You will flourish in this season of your fruitfulness. Watch and see and believe with all your heart. You will ride above the world that has held you at bay for so long."

A 24/7 VOICE

This is a season of restoration for the people of God. Do some study and write about it; write about what part forgiveness plays in it. 2 Kings 19:30 has been a powerful verse for me. Trust God's right time and place for you to put down roots. The roots have to be down, in good ground, to bear fruit upward. If you are frustrated that you don't see fruition, look at the roots you live with. Or without. God has a word for you, a good word as you want to go deeper in Him.

MANIFEST

"You are Lord over all time and happenings on earth. You are the fulfillment. Your people see like You do, from Your perspective. We walk together through this world where there is no breakthrough without You, and with You, all things are possible: past, present, and future."

PART 2

GOING
DEEPER

PROPHETIC PREPARATION

"Therefore let all the faithful pray to you while
you may be found; surely the rising of the
mighty waters will not reach them."

PSALM 32:6

DAY 8
REAL TIME, ETERNAL NOW

When God reaches for you with revelation, you have to be watching for it. Do you know why? An alarm goes off in the enemy's headquarters. The threat you used to be has now been magnified. He sends out reinforcements to try to fog your vision enough for you to doubt, forget, or miss it. The time to pray when an issue comes to view or into mind is NOW, so you can intercept the enemy's attempt to kill, steal, or destroy the Word as it comes with life; and so you can receive all God has in store for you.

I spent years stuck in the past, thinking I could do nothing about what happened. I'd climb out of the *past* and then I'd fly forward, *past* present, and think about the future with fear. Day after day, back and forth, past, future, past, future. **This is enemy interception of God's prophetic intentions for you.**

I used to think zeroing in on what happened *back there* and how it impacted me was the epitome of "going deeper" . . . after all, it is in psychological circles. But so much for circles: I was tired of going around and around and getting deeper entrenched. I took His word as Truth and began demanding my mind cast down empty vain imaginations. That's a present tense activity that *must* become your established habit. Commit 2 Corinthians 10:5 to memory! Your mind and emotions are as precious to God as your spirit. Close every door to your enemy by renewing your mind (Rom. 12:1, 2) and pray in the Spirit language you've been given (Eph. 6:18).

Moving from temporal to eternal

It's an amazing walk with God that takes a human being in earth time into the eternal now with God. Two Real-Time changes we'll explore today lift us into a closer walk with God's Third Heaven atmosphere. In His Eternal Now, we can "reckon it to be so" before ever seeing it. Sounds prophetic to me.

When you read a Biblical reference to eternal time and earth time, it sounds something like this: "Likewise reckon ye also yourselves to be dead indeed unto sin, but alive unto God through Jesus Christ our Lord." (Rom. 6:11) What has been eternally finished doesn't look yet like it's accomplished at all, but it's the realest accomplishment going in our lives! It's about believing God's eternal action transcending earth events. Let's go here today.

First, acknowledging we are citizens of heaven becomes a real location change in a spiritual sense. The Greek word for *heaven* is *"ouranos,"* which means *heaven* or **eternity**. It's where God is. But it *isn't where satan lives anymore!* He was cast out of there. Get it? That means your enemy has **no business** in the eternal realm from where God expresses His life to us! Satan is stuck in earth time, forever thrown out of the *ouranos*. The only way he can deter this calamity (for him) is to stop it in earth time from *your* vantage point! In your head . . . in your thought life . . . trying to cast a lie as truth: and if you believe it, he has every intention of bringing it into real time. You can see now why God says to take every thought captive to the obedience of Christ! (2 Cor. 10:5) Do you see what this verse in its prophetic truth takes you to?

Where in this process **do you stand? In the** *ouranos:* "And hath raised us up together, and made us sit together in heavenly places in Christ Jesus" (Eph. 2:6) Walking out this heavenly position above the things of the world will *change* the times we live in. That's what obedience to His Word produces, and we need to see this as a real result that impacts the days of our lives.

The second time change into eternal present comes with what Bible teacher, Perry Stone, calls these days in which scripture is being fulfilled on almost a daily basis, **"prophetic time crunch."** For so long the elements of what makes up an epic event are *being laid in place.* Every day while it's called today, actions and intentions are being done to effect change for the future. Listen, this applies to your life, too! It's the way things come to pass. It takes time and interactions, people, nations, seasons, and many moves of things unseen, including the Spirit of God. As the time for prophetic fulfillment approaches, **the**

events that need to be fulfilled start happening *closer and closer* to each other. The "fullness of times" is how the Bible puts it, and when it is "time," **it happens. In Real Time.** Today. It just happened. And now it's *news*? Eternal present has just revealed itself to our human eyes.

Heaven coming to earth has always been real time, eternal now

The birth of Messiah was prophesied by God's Word, seeded into the Jews' world in those words for thousands of years. Yet, it happened unexpectedly to most everyone, except for those *who were watching for it.* The world was forever changed. The Old Testament was consummated and a New Covenant with God was birthed, and the plan of God leapt forward! It was spoken of in the past, but it was the game changer the moment it happened. From there, the future stills plays out till all things are completed according to all God has initiated from the beginning (in Genesis 1). They are *eternity* played out today, in our Real Time.

"Prophetic Time Crunch" happened *in a day* in the re-birth of the nation of Israel after 2,500 years of having been "no longer a nation." Yet, it had been prophesied hundreds of times and ways by numerous writers of the Old Testament. Imagine that! There remain more biblical prophecies and at least one more major fulfillment of epic scriptural proportion, and we will see our Savior as he touches the Mount of Olives.

I spent years thinking that because He was soon to return that I shouldn't invest in this temporal season called my life. He spoke to me through parables about talents and lampstands, and also in His words to my spirit. He made time valuable to me.

"This is exactly the time for you to move in power: today! To finish up what I put in you! It is not time to fall asleep in sorrow, fear or hopelessness. It's not time to start 'eating and drinking for tomorrow we will die.' Today, while it is today, means now. This is the very season to gird up your heart and soul. If you think, 'The longer time goes on, the more desperately you need Me' is a bad thing, what will you think when I AM all that can help you? Every day, you're in this race; don't you dare stop needing Me; don't you dare stop running with me just because it's uphill from here! **It's what I have been pre-**

paring you for, and it is what your heart has looked toward all these years! Child, I am *excited* about, even *passionate* for, what I am going to do in these hours before the end of the age. For soon this battle will be spiritual history for My people. It is time to *rejoice*, not go back to the old life. Your old life is dead, but you are alive in Me forever!"

A 24/7 VOICE

Living in Eternal Now lifts us above the enemy's strategies to take us down: he no longer has access to eternal power, but *we* do in Christ! *Freedom*! *Rejoicing*! Write it out, this journey you've been on. Prophesy to your own heart about Today, real time, *God's eternal now,* in us.

MANIFEST

"I have a real-time relationship with You, God! I will not stop crying out for more of You! I have such a sense of expectancy and, yes, even joy. Meet with Me Lord and help me turn over everything to You so I can walk in Your eternal Now."

DAY 9
FIRE INSIDE

Many people of God, including the Biblical prophets, have said God looks at judgment as being a way to wake up sleeping people. By shaking us awake, God finally gets our attention, lest we be like the frog in the frying pan as it keeps heating up. I surely hope you and I have not been sleeping. Yet, if we have been, He knows how to wake us up. If you're going through some hefty trials, respond to Him aggressively and desperately! What's He after from you? He wants the allegiance of your heart, out of the world and hidden in Him. (Rev. 18:4) Only Real Time in His presence will get you there: real relationship, real honesty, real and whole hearted action. None of that lukewarm stuff. It's far too late for that, so give it up. Today we're going to kindle that fire inside!

When we're desperate for Him, God moves in, but not because He wanted to hear us beg or that He's finally weary of our wailing. In the heat of our desperately pressing in to His Spirit, the ground between us becomes a holy place where the enemy has a hard time traversing. It's too hot for him! This lifestyle makes us stronger, and that's exactly what God is after, for our good. Look with me at this verse that has two related and connected meanings. "And from the days of John the Baptist until now, the kingdom of heaven suffers violence, and the violent take it by force." This verse spoken by Jesus and found in Matthew 11:12 is also to be translated this way: "**The kingdom of heaven has been forcefully advancing and forceful men lay hold of it.**" This change of perspective is a powerful one: **it is the kingdom of heaven, not the kingdom of darkness that is advancing forcefully!** This is a clash that we can feel. You need to know *you're on the winning side if you are in Christ!* Mind you, this battle will be accomplished in real time, every day. Is it getting hot in here or is it just me?

As time winds out things start happening quickly. **Over the centuries** a nation and a world gradually become wicked. But when the whole system is "done," it limps along economically for only a few more decades until the cup of wickedness is full and the tipping point is poised for that one last thing. Then it can come down in a day . . . John's Revelation says, in *one hour!* (Rev. 18:10) **That's not much time to prepare if you're waiting for a really big sign or have ignored the ones that have been in your face.**

Today, the world is poised for many things: economic collapse, famine, earthquakes, oceans dying, rulers willing to sacrifice millions of lives for their purposes; death and destruction, nuclear threat, and even calamities from the heavens, such as asteroids. It's all been spoken of in the Bible thousands of years ago. It's been going on for many centuries. Yet today is indeed different, don't let anyone take from you the sense of suspense: it's there for a reason. When we deaden our spiritual sense, a vital part of us is rendered powerless. Let's get ready now by going deeper into this practical, powerful, prophetic relationship in Jesus.

What has you fired up inside? What events or situations cause you to think hard or get riled up? What is it that really gets you upset? **These areas are clues as to how God wants to move in on you to be a help and to see you into a new season of victory in the midst of trouble.**

The Church has this growing and electrifying anticipation of the end of the age. It's going to be sooner than we think . . . I think. It's driving us to seek God more thoroughly, obey quicker, reach out faster, and let go of what has held us back for so long. Or, at least it should. We now **need God's supernatural life** like never before. Guess what? It is ours to walk into if you're ready to go deeper.

> *Like Paul, we can consider our lives and troubles but a small*
> *thing for the excellency of the knowledge of Christ.*

It's God's Holy Spirit Power at work in us that provokes and empowers us to action. *Our desperate grasp on God* exerts a choke-hold on the enemy and our Spirit-inspired declarations bind him. This process of submitting to God, standing in faith, resisting the enemy, loving, and believing, *is the Holy Ghost's furnace of fire.* When the useless vanity of life is burned out, His altar is a holy fire for the saints of God. The Spirit is getting His bride to a place where our default complaint is, like Jeremiah groaned, "But if I say, 'I will not mention his word or speak anymore in his name,' his word is in my heart like a fire, a fire shut up in my bones. I am weary of holding it in; indeed, **I cannot.**" (Jer. 20:9) Man, it's really feeling hot in here.

Here's the beauty of going through *this* kind of heavenly fire: our hearts, motives and desires open to God's touch, our spiritual eyes open, our supernatural hearing opens . . . and God's heaven opens. **Open Ears. Open Eyes. Open Heaven.** He will not withhold any good thing from them that love Him enough to seek Him out. It's at that point we can see the prophetic working all along in us, to will and work and do of His good pleasure. He promises that we will be overcomers if we let Him work in us and we continue to stand: not just overcomers of tiny insignificant stuff, but overcomers of catastrophes, hordes, adversities and all the fiery darts of the wicked one! It's the supernatural life we need and want, and *need to want,* more and more. Get ready, the fire of the Holy Spirit is coming before Messiah's Second Coming.

We can come boldly to the throne of grace. Isn't it *prophetic:* What you have burning in your heart for three decades as a hope and desire is quite likely the very thing God put in there and is fanning in your heart till it bursts into flames. If things feel more intense to you these days, check and see if it's feeling hot in there (point to your heart). Maybe it's time to open the oven door and let the dream out.

A 24/7 VOICE

If you've had a set of circumstances you're tempted to allow to get in the way of this practical powerful prophetic life, Paul had already gotten his attitude adjustment when he wrote: "And I, brethren, when I came to you, came not with excellency of speech or of wisdom, declaring unto you the testimony of God. For I determined not to know anything among you, save Jesus Christ, and him crucified." (1 Cor. 2:1, 2) Nothing stopped him. He kept it simple. Today, nothing need stop you. Answer to the fire inside. Let everything else fall away, where it needs to go. Write about this in an acrostic. Here's one example, using the word, HOPE, as a grid:

Here are my ears, God,
Open them! Right now I'm
Probably running on
Empty until they hear You

You say, *how can that be helpful*? **Now, it is God's turn to speak.** Pray in the Holy Ghost toward this end. Find scripture and meditate on it. Listen and write. Let His Spirit have the last word. And be filled.

MANIFEST

"God, You are the fire inside Your people. Fire me up; I declare I will see You for real; see Your hand work on my behalf; hear Your voice speak in my inner man. If need drives me to You, then it also is the element and spark for strength to come. Need will also drive me into the world to share Your goodness. Hallelujah."

DAY 10
ROOT CAUSES

et's go back in time to our spiritual roots. What I relate here is
strategically important to our spiritual walk, our prophetic
"take" and the outworking of Holy Spirit in all areas of our lives.
I've made mention of these things before now but today we have
more ground laid in place to grow our prophetic spirit strong. **There
are two camps from which spiritual things come forth.** Yes, we're
going to The Garden, the first garden that eventually necessitated the
second one, where drops of blood fell into the earth and watered the
ground of the new creation called the Church. This whole idea about
good and evil has been a tricky business. It was God who determined
the parameters of good and evil, but someone else horned in.

The two opposing camps are described in terms of **trees.** Scripturally and symbolically, trees and wood usually refer to human beings
and the essence of what makes man who he is in his humanness.
Think of a tree, then, as a *source* of growth, building, strength, provision, and expansion. First, there is **the Tree of Life** which belongs to
God alone; it is about life in God's Spirit, which is eternal and true
life. It grows fruit and is for healing (Rev. 22).

The second is **the Tree of the Knowledge of Good *and* the
Knowledge of Evil.** This other "tree" is not only about the *knowledge*
of *good*, as you can read, but it also holds, "the *knowledge* of *evil*." It is
about *knowledge*: a lot of knowledge, all jumbled up and growing together in one tree, good and bad, from one trunk. Imagine, good and
evil indistinguishable? It is an avalanche of knowledge, a tsunami
of it, a mudslide of it. Words upon words, upon words of knowledge. So much information, in fact, that The Truth is made to look
like just another 60 second commercial on TV, washed away by the

programs surrounding it. You may have seen it recently on your own big-screen.

The world has mountains of unending options about what you might want to think about, see, do, remember, entertain, ingest, commit to memory, enjoy, gloat over, and live off of, into, and for . . . and you can also believe any or all of it is the truth if you want to. "It's *your* truth." As far back as history and then some, we now have access to all the knowledge of good and the knowledge of evil we could not even *possibly* imagine. It's all right there online at our fingertips. How convenient.

Adam and Eve already had *God's* mind on every matter, all they needed to know, including what to do with those two trees. What more powerful way to introduce a lie than to whisper half-truths? Eve was confused when she heard the serpent (the whisperer, the accuser) *when his words sounded positively prophetic to her*! Both Adam and Eve's Real-time with God should have produced a markedly better response than for them to believe the lie.

Neither you nor I would have done any better a job. In fact, it wasn't too long ago I was shown a response that matched theirs in the garden.

> I dreamed about being in a group of people I knew well. They were all in the process of doing their thing, busy, except for one person who was laying on a couch. As I walked by, I made a snide remark about him being a couch potato, and at that moment a Pastor came right over to me and said, *What did you say?* She tried to hand me a dollar. The dollar kept showing up and I refused it.

Her trying to hand me a dollar was a gesture of, *"here is the price for you to cease and desist this slanderous attitude."* Ouch. It was one dollar because when sin presents itself, it may look like a small thing, like one apple on a tree. But sin (like leaven) amounts to a lot! It can ruin a person and then, many people; a church; a marriage; a life; generations: *it's not worth it*. "A little leaven" was in my heart. (Gal. 5:9) We know who paid the ultimate price for sin: to have to face Him with my castigation of a brother He died for was heart breaking. I was so upset I woke up: my fallen nature was found out right then and there, because the Spirit of God had free reign in that place in my dream. I recalled the dream and realized I wasn't even sure where the root of this attitude was lodged, or how long it had been there.

> The Lord said, *"It doesn't matter at this moment where or how long. I'll show that to you.* **Right now, simply repent and take authority over the spirit it has traveled in. Demand it leave forever."* So I did. I *felt* nothing but I saw an image of a ground out of which a long root system had been removed. I asked, *What will happen to that empty space where the roots were?* He said, *Would you like to plant something else in there, or leave it open, or allow Me to fill it?* That was a loaded question but it got straight to the root of how we invite "plants" (play on words) other than God to take up residence and put down roots in our attitude.

The tree of the knowledge of good and the knowledge of evil was never supposed to be what people derive **life** from. Yet if we aren't watchful we'll still live there today, even without knowing it . . . until the Spirit of prophecy reveals to you what needs rooting out.

Everything God ever did has been prophetic; it still is and always will be, because that is who and how He is.

Right from the start this Book of God, the Bible, is prophetic! No wonder the world stumbles over its contents. No wonder a world under the influence of the evil one calls the miraculous things Holy Spirit does and wants to do in us *obsolete, ridiculous, unnecessary, presumptuous, and even ungodly.* When we hear these accusations then we know we are listening to the serpent.

> These are the days I AM uprooting the roots of this tree, of the knowledge of good and the knowledge of evil, whose roots have vexed the earth underneath and whose branches have grown a web over the sky. I AM planting the people of God firmly in the Tree of Life. I AM clearing the land, wiping the sky, and trimming the tree for the approach of My Kingdom! When you see the land cleared and the sky wiped it will look like devastation. The Kingdoms of the world will be cleared, and the sky wiped clean, and then will come the Glorious Kingdom. This is the season, children. Hold fast and grow in the Good Ground. Put your roots down deep in the Tree of Life that never dies and bear much fruit upwards to the glory of My Name. For I come quickly, *soon*, and we shall rule and reign together.

I heard these words, then a sudden vision surfaced. I wondered why something so positive as this word I just heard had to be followed by something fallen! It was a vision of a teenager's bedroom: *trashed* with months, maybe seasons of clothes, rumpled and dirty, mashed together with half eaten food on dirty plates, books, forks and paper napkins wadded up, electronics, bags, sports stuff, and random unnamed items. A lamp is overturned, curtains are half closed, and the bed is almost invisible under the heap of stuff all over it. It all spells disregard, distraction, and disarray. *The room was so trashed that no one could know if an intruder had come in and walked away with something valuable* unless they searched through the whole mess. He took me back to root causes being entrenched in sin. The thought came to me: It's a real bummer when you've been robbed and don't know it because you didn't regard what you had as something to be valued. Like Esau giving up his birthright for a bowl of soup. Like the Parable of the Ten Virgins. Like godliness in our culture, or a loving attitude toward a brother in Christ. You can't say we haven't been warned. And you can't say we don't have a mighty help either. All that from the roots of sin still entrenched in our lives until a revelation comes our way and God helps us see.

A 24/7 VOICE

Time for a little art in your journal. Get ready to wax creative. Maybe use crayons for that. You need space for 2 trees. On the left page, the tree of life. On the right page, the tree of the knowledge of good and the knowledge of evil. (What part does the word *knowledge* play?) Are any of the branches of the 2 trees connected? Make this as **prophetic** a picture as you can. And enjoy this; it is not a punishment.

MANIFEST

"God is the God of the tree of Life. If there are any roots in me that have to be plucked out in order for Your voice to come through loud and clear, then pluck away, my God! God's people reject every form of deception that could lead them away from You."

DAY 11
AWAKE TO RIGHTEOUSNESS

God has been close in our lives for the entire time we've been on earth. Dreams we've had as children often turn out to speak to us of future things: our direction, our calling, the earth's future and developing events. The deeper we go into God's Spirit, the more awake we are to righteousness. Getting ready for miracles means we must value God's ways above man's ways. You know the old saying, "she's so heavenly minded she's no earthly good"? That's not a *true* saying. When we become more heavenly minded, we can finally become more earthly good. **It's the switch to faith in our supernatural God that gets us ready for miracles.** It's this switch to faith in His Word that gives us the victory over our flesh and the enemy of our souls. How long has that message been rolling around in my own head, I wonder.

"I was walking toward a thick patch of forest. It was dark around me, like twilight, but I knew it was day. I entered the woods and made a way through till I suddenly came to a steep open hillside before me. It was veiled in shadow on this side, and it rolled down to a stream far below. Across the stream on the other side, the steep hill climbed up. That side of the hill was bathed in sparkling sunlight and brilliant colors. At the top of the other side was a house; I knew I was to go there. I continued down, crossed over, and came up. Immediately I found myself in the house, in the kitchen, at a small table with two chairs facing each other. I climbed up into the chair closest to me. As I faced the table I realized *God was in the other seat!* I couldn't see Him, but I surely knew, as if I knew Him already. There He was, welcoming me into His presence! I felt His Fatherly acceptance and love, and felt completely at peace; He was no stranger, nor was I to Him. He spoke to me and I understood I was meant to live with Him, for He had already adopted me. Filled with joy, and with that part settled, I suddenly saw on the left arm of the chair in which I was sitting, a huge snake. Slowly and silently it was winding up the arm towards me, with "intent to kill." Before I could become afraid, I heard these words from Father: "You do not have to be afraid of him." Then I woke up.

Though this prophetic dream introduced me to the Truth, it didn't register in my brain as something to ponder for a long time. One thing we have to understand about the supernatural: revelation does not come *from* our brain, but it eventually *gets to* our brain. Though I wasn't cognitively aware of it, this dream revealed
8 Elementary Scriptural Truths:

1. The Fatherhood of God
2. The plan of salvation
3. That we have an enemy
4. What this enmity means to the Kingdom of God
5. That I had decisions to make: to cross over from a life in the darkness, to the light
6. That I had to choose to enter His household and live there
7. It cemented the fact that I needed a total re-location of my life
8. And because God said so, we do not have to fear

It's a simple to understand dream; and it's a good thing, too: I don't think I was even five years old when I had it. It has stayed with me all my life, part of the foundational understanding God must whisper into hearts early on in life. There was a battle for me. But in the long run, this dream sowed seeds from the Tree of Life into a ground birthed initially in the other tree.

We are invited to share the lively hope God has that everyone will awake to righteousness

Long before I knew God as my Father; long before I gave my life to Him, this dream was with me. I would submit to you today that there are hundreds of people all around us who don't profess Jesus at this time; *but in their dreams they have heard Him, seen Him, and learned something from Him.* God may already have given us the key that opens them to Jesus *through their own memory.*

Isn't that what Daniel did when he interpreted the dream Nebuchadnezzar couldn't even remember? (Dan. 2) Even today, the revelations in Daniel's centuries-old experience with dreams and visions are *still coming to bear* on you, me, and the world. *Those dreams Daniel heard from God were also for these days today.* Imagine that! Ancient dreams in Real-time acceleration toward completion. That's the power of the prophetic action of God, past, present, and future.

Imagine, I might have gone to sleep to dream *and awakened to righteousness,* all in one 24 hour period, had I known I could! That's the value of instruction by wiser adults. That's the importance of hearing truth in our inward parts. That's what revelation accomplishes when allowed to bring forth the fruit it is intended to bear. That's what Spirit-filled churches are for.

After my introductory dream, it took many years for me to give Him my heart. But the enemy couldn't stop what God had started. Jesus headed him off at the cross-road of my life. The intersection of God's timing, the perfect place, and many other elements simply ushered Jesus into my heart forever. Or ushered me into His heart. It was actually through another dream when the working of the cross finally became life to me. In 1972 the dream He sent me was an encounter to this effect:

> I saw the Lord walking toward me over a bridge. I had no recollection of having ever seen Him before but I knew it was the Lord. As He was halfway over the walkway, I said, *I can't do this. What I've done is too bad.* My words stopped Him for a minute and then He smiled! He asked me, 'Is what I've done not enough?' I woke up suddenly. I'd never had a dream like this before, so personally addressed to me. All I could focus on was the lack of anger and the presence of joy. And that smile!

God-sent, prophetic dreams help wake us to righteousness in some way, shape, or form. God wants to reveal the hidden things (2 Cor.) to us so we will have *that* also as our strong foundation. We get to have dreams, visions, people speaking into our lives prophetically, and the Spirit of love to help us turn our thinking to right ways without feeling condemned. He positively sparks our lives with the *dunamis* power of Holy *alive* Spirit! It's the most wonderful wake-up call ever invented! "... for the light makes everything visible. This is why it is said, 'Awake, O sleeper, rise up from the dead, and Christ will give you light'." (Eph. 5:14 NLT)

A 24/7 VOICE

Write out your first ever interaction with God. How old were you, what happened? How is your walk with God different now, both positive and negative? Put a title at the top of the page, maybe words you find from a newspaper or magazine, cut out, and/or pieced together. **Consider every creative operation a prophetically meaningful action.** Do this practice with the understanding that you will meet up with someone and help them awake to righteousness through the sharing of something that has happened to you prophetically: God telling you something in a dream, or a revelation, etc.

MANIFEST

"Hallelujah, I woke up when I least expected it! Your faithfulness retrieves the lost, the sleeping, the dead. Help me speak into everyone's lives with the same kind of prophetic life You sent into mine! Truth is Who You are, and Your servant is who I am!"

DAY 12
REVELATION GENERATION

Everyone can live in God's presence. That's His invitation in Christ. The gift of revelation refers to God blessing us with spiritually tuned inner vision in which we perceive His wishes, intentions, and heart on a personally directing level. Without this gift we cannot even think we are invited into God's presence. Though not everyone is "called to be" a prophet, everyone filled with the Spirit of God may prophesy. My aim is to nudge you to seek Him *for more, for deeper, for all* He has for you to glorify Him. In His presence, that's where you belong.

The New Testament shows us that the prophetic words God speaks can come through anyone baptized and living immersed in the Holy Spirit. (1 Cor. 14:1, 2) Today, the Spirit's intention for the prophetic is to build up, to enable healing to flow, and to encourage, keep, and direct that which belongs to God. (1 Cor. 14:4, 5) It requires us to live humble and teachable, and that comes from obeying what we learn in His presence. He has been known to send His word through donkeys when no human was willing to submit to God in the prophetic moment. (Num. 22:21–39) Though prophetic life is like learning to walk a new way, it's not reserved for a select few anymore. Jesus opened the way for this new creation: and in each new creation it takes some practice.

- Holy Spirit helps us begin a spiritual **practice** that develops our seeing and hearing. "My sheep hear My voice and I know them and they follow Me." (John 10:27)
- We learn different **"love-languages"** with God as we learn to hear His voice

- We have a potentially 24/7 **appointed meeting**. We can **expect to hear** from Him constantly, just like He wants to hear from us constantly

It's similar to a human relationship with someone you're in covenant with. Imagine being married. Imagine that all the communication you have had with your spouse is the letter they wrote to you when they were introduced to you. All thirty years you have been living in "wedded bliss," your spouse never once talked to you face to face, whispered in your ear what only you should hear; never wrote you a personal love note on a post-it and put it where you'd find it; didn't call, text, or even look you in the eye? It's the same sort of situation regarding relationship with Holy Spirit: it is a big mistake to think we can't or don't need intimate communication with Him every day. It's a big loss. But I believe, "This *is* the generation of them that seek him, that seek thy face, O Jacob. Selah." (Ps. 24:6)

Holy Spirit speaks out: A 24/7 Voice for ears that want to hear

Revelation comes prophetically, and it reveals something you need to know courtesy of the One who spoke it into your spirit. It can happen like this: you read the Bible for hours at a time, same scriptures, and then one day, *kapow*! It suddenly springs to life! The word that used to be ho-hum or merely cerebrally approved of, becomes real, alive, pertinent, and powerful! In Greek we say it happened this way: the *logos* becomes *rhema*. What were once words we could make sense of mentally, at least, now become full of transforming life! They're no longer words *to* you, they are *in you*! *Yours*! It seems in an instant everything is different. *Rhema* Word takes on a new tone, incorporating this new and lively revelation into the fabric of the whole.

> Seek Me with an attitude of receptivity. I Am the opening up of your understanding in the midst of situations you are in. Suddenly, you'll be standing at the window and see something outside that speaks in your spirit! Or you'll zoom in on something in someone's conversation that strikes you as "odd." When you're alert to these moments, when they happen, they won't just slip by as random thoughts that have no relevancy. Ask Me for My wisdom, for I have it for you! Be *ready* to hear the Spirit of your Lord answer.

Practice how Jeremiah saw God's message. God asked him, "Jeremiah, what do you see?" Then he looked and saw. He noticed something in particular. It wasn't a vision. It was a learning time with God using something seen to explain something to come.

Look around and find an object somewhere that draws your attention to ruminate on: in the kitchen, on the porch, as you drive down a highway. Like Jesus using parables to explain something spiritual, ask for God to speak to you about some subject He wants to touch on. In regard to that subject, look around with your eyes waiting to see it expounded on in an object or event. The prophetic answer builds our faith and prepares us for the next door God opens. If that is a troublesome time or a time of blessing and abundance, we will be ready because He has prefaced it with His own words and illustration.

All forms of the prophetic, dreams and visions included, are meant to accomplish five important facets of His nature and will:

1. *Reveal* God's direction, warning for safety
2. *Provide* God's change-order or redirected trajectory
3. *Know* His encouragement, wisdom and revelation on behalf of
4. *Share* of His comfort, solace, and healing
5. *Show* that God is who He says He is in every way

By His Spirit He can drop a word in our hearts. It could be to work with Him as He moves in the world to impact whole nations. Instead of us feeding on fear of famine, He can raise us up to feed multitudes by faith! Why should that surprise us? He has provided the prophetic gifts for all His children for purposes like these. Listen to and see needs, and *don't ignore them.* Ignoring needs will only train you to not look, or when you do look, **not see!**

There could easily be a God-inspired idea, help, or fix that wouldn't have seen the light of day had you not taken the idea seriously and prophetically. **Begin to build your expectation level of what God's intentions are** for you in this coming season. When the Son of Man returns He wants to find faith. (Luke 18:8)

You don't want to miss it

A little trouble in the world never has stopped God. Here in this eleventh hour, prophetically speaking, even if we aren't sure whether this is the day to "look up, for our redemption draweth nigh," or, that we should gird ourselves up for the Last Battle—or the Big Revival—or the downfall of the USA and the upsurge of our enemies—or God's blessing on His people—or the implosion of our economy, or the "abomination that maketh desolate" (Matt. 24:15)—or *all the above at one time*—**we *can* be sure our faithful God will keep us**! He will keep us informed; keep us on the cutting edge; keep us abreast of how He wants to move in any season night or day, 24/7. That's why this is the Revelation Generation.

A 24/7 VOICE

Recount a time when the Lord fulfilled a Word from the Bible right in your life. Write a prayer that comes to you as you remember how sweet that type of fellowship is in your heart. Listen, because He wants to take you to another place with Him, another time of fellowship. If you can go for a walk, why not? Meditate on John 14:16,17 and write your thoughts.

MANIFEST

"I declare that I receive revelation from You and that I hear right things. You open my eyes to see around me, to see and meet needs through Your Spirit. I'm learning to expect Your Words to produce what You sent them to produce! So be it!"

DAY 13
POSERS AND PROPHETS

Not all who call themselves Christian, are. Jesus warned, "Many will say to me in that day, Lord, Lord, have we not prophesied in thy name? And in thy name have cast out devils? And in thy name done many wonderful works? And then will I profess unto them, I never knew you: depart from me, ye that work iniquity." (Matt. 7:22, 23) His answer jars me! It sounds like there's a distinct possibility I could only be thinking I am obeying Him, when I'm actually doing as I please! The time to discover that would be *now* and not later. I keep that attitude in mind a lot these days, as "it's dangerous out there."

This is the place for a trust level and relationship that goes deeper and calls us higher:

> It's impossible to walk in the revelation of Christ-in-you and the manifestation of the sons of God while living a shoddy, selfish spiritual walk. That is why I will never be One to allow your flesh to rule you. You may choose that, but if you belong to Me, I will work to realign your calling as a king and priest. I love you.
>
> Remember who I AM to you when you are tempted to get lazy, distracted, or neglectful. The fallen world you live in will always call for you to return, to devolve, to dissolve our ties. This is the season of the supernatural power of God to be manifested in My people, so you know the enemy will want to sabotage such a promise, as it means he is bound!
>
> Enter into a deeper place where we commune face to face so you do not "accidentally" walk away. We are not ignorant of the enemy's devices.

I AM well able to keep you as long as your heart 'demands it as
a vital necessity'. A willing heart will grow strong in My will. Trust Me,
I will keep you if you trust Me and put no faith in the flesh.

God wants every person to be free in His Spirit to live out His
calling, and fully persuaded in their own mind (Rom. 14:5) so there is
no room for subterfuge, lukewarmth, pretense or lies. We can't walk
this practical, powerful prophetic under cover of darkness. We are
lights of a city set on a hill . . . a city surrounded by God's angels . . .
whose builder and maker is God.

So today, after two weeks learning that our range of hearing is far
greater than we guessed, can we go there to examine our hearts, to
know and be known, so His ways can be what we are really serving?

Below are **7 Biblically-based Criteria for How Father God Sees**
world issues and the people involved in them. They are parameters
and guides for living prophetically:

1. God hates no person; He is love
2. But He hates any sin that will end up taking them to an
   eternal death
3. **He sent His Son to go to the cross** for *every* person, for all
   time, *while* we yet hated Him
4. Because He is God and God is love, He *alone* has the first and
   last word on what works for human beings: He *is* the *only*
   Word of Truth
5. You have to believe in Him and know Jesus Christ in personal
   relationship to grasp this and not think He is either a tyrant
   or figment
6. If people hate Christians, they should understand that means
   they hate God
7. Regardless what any person thinks, God's Word doesn't *have*
   to change. It started out as the Truth and it continues to stand
   as the original and only stand-alone Truth, forever

Compromise is spiritual suicide for everyone: Christians miss the
best of the best, and unbelievers never begin believing better. The
enemy's attempt to make posers is by keeping them from growing.
There are whole churches and denominations that *deny the veracity of*

the entirety of God's Word: Old and New Testaments included; Holy Spirit indwelling, miracles, tongues and interpretation of tongues, the supernatural and prophetic included; presuming that they in this special group are above certain of His words . . . on and on. The church's compromise becomes the peoples' sin.

Find a church where Holy Spirit is welcome, where the Word is held as final authority, and things are still done decently and in order, a church that is grounded in the five-fold ministry that will equip and establish you in the *whole Truth* and that will help you develop in your giftings, not hold you back. There, if you have a willing and obedient heart, you will grow and thrive.

We have reached the two week point in hearing God's 24/7 voice. You're created, called, and chosen to live like a prophet, not a poser. Re-cap the last two weeks: we have a God, a calling, a guarantee, a fullness, an eternal perspective, a perfect timing, a real time relationship, godly and accurate discernment. And so much more.

> *"We also have the prophetic message as something completely reliable, and you will do well to pay attention to it, as to a light shining in a dark place, until the day dawns and the morning star rises in your hearts."* (2 Pet. 1:19)

A 24/7 VOICE

Go back to the paragraph, **How God our Father looks at world issues.** In thinking about the problems the world is immersed in, can you see a different approach your Spirit-filled life can take to reach someone who might not like you very much because you're a Christian with godly values? It might not be easy. It might get you in trouble. But it might touch their heart to feel a new way about God's reach to them. Write it as if you were teaching it to a student. That means, Explain. Explain from God's heart and not your understanding. Describe how prayer is an important part of hearing accurately.

MANIFEST

"I could get disgusted with myself for letting things slip by that end up sabotaging me! But instead, I push through in faith to lay hold on Your nature for my sustenance and life. Take me further than I've been willing to go up till now. I refuse to be a poser."

DAY 14
SPIRIT OF TRUTH, SPIRIT OF ERROR

In the media and news, not a day goes by without reports of failing economies, terrorism, the movements of people groups across borders, breaking down of relationships at every level, murder, wickedness increasing unabated, threats of pandemic, famine, communication breakdowns through lies, imminent nuclear war, a one-world government, and the last ditch attempts to destroy Israel. It's easy to see how people can be desensitized to all this violence and upheaval. You'll hear their dismissals of end times with comments like, "There are so many more people in the world today it only seems like a lot worse is happening"; "Bad things have always happened"; and "Technology enables us to know everything so fast now, it's not like it used to be, hearing of disasters three weeks later." Biblically, *these are prophetic times in present tense*.

We have a choice how we handle this intel. Now is not the time to give up or gripe. Now, we pray. We stand. We send reinforcements to the troops in battle, especially spiritual battle. If we can, we support and supply those in the middle of the crisis.

We will watch closely and "listen to see" what the Lord will say: "I will stand at my watch and station myself on the ramparts; I will look to see what he will say to me, and what answer I am to give to this complaint." (Hab. 2:1) We can know what is coming because we know the one who has it all under control. "Indeed, the Sovereign LORD never does anything until he reveals his plans to his servants the prophets." (Amos 3:7 NLT) These words are not just for the prophets who received the first word. They are God's reminder that as He continues to move prophetic events closer to fulfillment, His servants, the twenty-first century prophets will be hearing God's 24/7

Voice and reporting on it. Are you listening? Are you in a church that has prophetic intercessors that honor biblical prophecy as a practical powerful help in the congregation? The entirety of the Spirit of Truth is found in God's Word: it's just a lot larger, deeper, and more completely prophetic than we thought.

The Spirit of error, on the other hand, is trying to minimize and marginalize scriptural veracity and influence even within the church.

- It is accepting of a mixture of Christianity and other beliefs, thinking this will bring peace
- Claiming to serve God while they think all gods are the same is 180 degrees from what scripture says
- Claiming that the work of the cross was a failure and that we have to fix humanity on our own with the help of wise holy men outside the church

The true Body of Christ is still growing, and growing stronger. Growing stronger in China for example, stronger and more beautiful every day as the fire of God burnishes, perfects and transforms. You can hear powerful testimonies of Jesus in the Church in Africa, Indonesia, Iran, **in the world where you would not think the church could still possibly exist, given** *the fire* **they are in!** But in fact, they're standing, loving, and growing because they already counted the cost. There's no mixture there. They refuse to go underground, refuse to run, refuse to compromise. They rebuild. They grieve their dead who have gone to glory before they did. They go on reaching their people, and their enemies, with the news of Jesus. In the very places where God's Spirit is pressing into unreached people groups, the battle is immense and dangerous, and the Church is victoriously growing.

The fire of God can't be quenched. It just becomes more glorious

What turns a seemingly healthy church to one of mixture with the world?

- Not listening to God and His prophets
- Reducing God's Word to fit their own preferences
- Listening to the world and its prophets
- Getting lukewarm, like a Laodicean church

The spirit of the age is a lying spirit and it has introduced a toxic spiritual poison with its message, into truth, into the waters of life, into the church. I saw the effect of the power of the Lie in a short dream.

> I was walking through a mall that had windows to outside, and it was just about dark, both inside and outside. A young boy with dark skin and dark thick hair, cute as could be, came up to me with a crystal fishbowl. In it was one sparkling brilliant orange goldfish swimming around in a circle. The boy didn't speak to me, but he held out the bowl to me and gestured, "Do you want a beautiful fish?" I answered, "No thank you, no I don't." But he reached his hand, which I then saw was filthy, into the pure water. As he grabbed the fish, it died right in his hand.

Struck by this image of the child holding the sparkling bowl and how innocent he was, I asked the Lord, *But why did the fish die? The boy didn't intend for that to happen!* Holy Spirit indicated, **this is what deception is like. This is how living without discernment can be deadly.** This is why making right selections by the Spirit is strategically important.

People who are living in a world of lies don't always know they are living in it. They may be sharers and promoters of death while thinking they are providing life. They reach into the realm of the spirit with unclean hands (because The Truth is not *the only Truth* to them) and the life dies. It doesn't take an avalanche of Lie, just a bit.

The reaching into unholy spirituality outside of Christ becomes deception; it becomes "strange fire," a spiritual allure that promises spiritual wisdom and motivation, but yields distancing from Jesus and spiritual death. Does it remind you of the lie first spoken in the Garden by the serpent? When you meet up with people who think their spiritual thoughts are as true as anyone else's, ask God for His wisdom to find the soft spot in their heart they thought they had anesthetized. They don't need to be denied the prophetic; they need to be introduced to The Truth, the testimony of Jesus, which is the Spirit of Prophecy. (Rev. 19:10)

At the same time this mixture is washing into the mainstream churches, the Spirit of Jesus is coming into meetings and people are being healed and set free. In worship, the atmosphere of heaven is bringing amazing praise and revelation. People are making the same decisions as those whose lives have been saved by Jesus in closed countries where to live is Christ and to die is next. This revelation generation crosses over the obstacles and lies to reach out to bear witness to the truth, even when the present is tense and so is the future. The Spirit of Truth trumps the spirit of error. We have one Truth: "And the Word became flesh and dwelt among us, and we beheld His glory, the glory as of the only begotten of the Father, full of grace and truth . . . but grace and truth came by Jesus Christ" (John 1:14, 17); "And ye shall know the truth, and the truth shall set you free." (John 8:32)

A 24/7 VOICE

"Look around you for the messages of the world and the messages of the Spirit of truth. How would you describe the difference? Are they always different on the surface? Look up the word "fire" (for fire of God) in your Concordance. Think about what is happening in your own life today that will impact your future. Listen. Read. Can you prophesy God's instructions in acrostic form? Use fire colors on your page.

MANIFEST

"Your Holy Fire is deepening in my heart to go through the fires of adversity. I will not fear, I will trust You, God. I will speak the truth in love. Your prophetic voice in me will lead me into all Truth."

PART 3
LIVING
WORDS

PROPHETIC AND POWERFUL

"Call to me and I will answer you and tell you great
and unsearchable things you do not know."

JEREMIAH 33:3

DAY 15
LIVING WATERS

"On the last day, that great day of the feast, Jesus stood and cried,
saying, If any man thirst, let him come unto me, and drink. He that
believeth on me, as the scripture hath said, out of his belly shall flow
rivers of living water. (But this spake he of the Spirit, which they
that believe on him should receive: for the Holy Ghost was not yet
given; because that Jesus was not yet glorified.)" (John 7:37–39)

J esus spoke these words prophetically before His own Spirit was sent to them. He was serious enough to cry, yes, and *express emotion* when He called the people to thirst for the rivers of living waters! He feels the same about this gift today. Of all people He knows the essential power it is while we live in the world: power to stand against temptation and the enemy, power to love and respond, power to do miracles, power to hear and see in the spirit, power to be conformed to His Spirit. His voice goes forth into the world and into the spiritual atmosphere around us to reach **whosoever will hear it.** Hearing is an active and transforming action.

This is what "living waters" looks like in the spirit: His voice speaks into the spirit of a man, because words are spiritual containers. It speaks to the inward man, it hits the conscience and provokes worship, it begins a process of intuitive thoughts. Living waters are the rain of the Holy Spirit. Living waters are a drenching rain. Living waters are a flood. They are a new tide coming in. But can you sense the urgency of the hour we live in? I've been in approaching hurricanes. It's ominous. It's a day of darkness and preparation. It's a day in which anything can happen and sometimes does.

I first started journaling years ago. But it was on the way into a hurricane of relationships being carried away from my life that I got really serious about it. Unfortunately I didn't have any strength to stand in the Word. That's why I am so verbal about it and about being ready for hard times.

I spent 90% of my journaling crying out my complaint before God. The 10% times when the Lord broke through my wails *with His words* of help, correction, and comfort, I was so smitten with His love and understanding, I knew I'd never doubt His ability to speak to me again. I learned the difference in our voices: My *pouring out* and *His pouring in* are two different things.

It is necessary to listen for **His voice *over* my own.** Our prophetic practice is to tune our ears to hear His "station." If we've given Him our ear and selected His station, we can hear better and more clearly in spite of static and storms.

Think of qualities of a river. A river's waters are always flowing, though it's not the same molecules passing by. They're connected, but fluid. They're the same body but different particles. What went by is gone but the same river is now "new" water. God is in the eternal "Now" . . . we can jump in any time, or never, or always, and He will be the same One True God and His Spirit always flows true.

So I want to ask: how do *you* "sense" the voice of Holy Spirit"? What does spiritual hearing behave like? I think of the water analogy again: I jump in, suddenly I get wet, the waves rush over me, I come up for air. These are right brain explanations that the left brain identifies as:

- Impressions, spontaneous, "suddenlies," a surprise revelation from what had simply been normal a moment before
- A new viewpoint or understanding: "I saw it in my mind, it was just *there*"
- Something I couldn't shake: "It was in my *gut*; I couldn't explain it, but I *knew*"

You notice these are not analytical or logical ways to "hear" from God. They don't come from the decision-making side of the brain. Revelation does not come *from* your brain, but it eventually *reaches* your brain. Impressions from the Spirit are intuitive, maybe even instinctual, while the mind is still trying to understand *how* this came to you. Here are two basic ways a **prophetic thought** appears to you personally while you are awake:

1. "Just a Word": Revelation may begin with one word or a single piece of advice: "Take heart." When we give it our attention, then revelation comes to us: ". . . **and here's where I want you to take it.**" This word has opened the door for Him to speak on. What comes next may be the living waters you were thirsting to hear.

2. "Trains of Thought": Revelation may be a long opening up of events that have happened, with a view toward wisdom and godly perspective. This could be in the form of a dream you've had, or a vision. But often it can and even should be a two way dialogue, with Him altering the course of your understanding process to adjust "trajectory." If you pursue this thought process and find it leading you to obsess, fear, despair, or confusion: ditch it. Take authority over your thoughts and cast them down as vain imaginations. Go back to the station, find The Conductor of your wisdom, and ask Holy Spirit for clarity.

We are in what you could call a "now" season! God is urgently calling to every person to come back to Him, come deeper into fellowship with Him, to put on His armor, receive His gifts, and walk in His fruits TODAY. Now. There can be no more mixing with worldviews, entertaining doubt, unbelief or disobedience. No more idolatry; no interfaith worship services where *all* the gods are honored and spoken to! He is not looking for the Laodicean Church: lukewarm, increased with goods, but blind, beggarly and naked spiritually. All these things are affronts to God, the God of Heaven.

He is looking for those who answer His heart call to bring in the Kingdom with Him. He calls for a holy people, set aside only for Him, upon whom He'll pour out this last and greatest outpouring of His power in these times. This has always been the message of course, but now the time is so short because **it's the end of the season** before He returns! This is the age of the harvest, not just by men's working to bring people to Christ, but the one harvested by the angels! (Rev.

14:15,19; Joel 3:13) Jesus would never have given the infilling indwelling Spirit so much press if being filled with His Spirit was something He would abolish after His ascension! Active, transforming *holiness* requires that we flow with His leading. We're not swimming against His current, we are being allowed to be led; filled, empowered, and led. Christ in us, our hope of glory! (Col. 1: 27)

A 24/7 VOICE

"I finally learned how to listen for His voice *over* my own." This is the Holy Spirit challenge you really want to take, it's so freeing. This process of knowing whose voice is whose is for our benefit, so when we desperately need to hear from Him we won't be so under the waters of adversity we can't hear clearly Who is over the waters. Write out your needs as we see the time coming ever closer to His return. Try an acrostic or acronym using the word RETURN.

MANIFEST

"I declare that I will not miss You when You speak. I will hear with my whole heart so that every moment becomes a new NOW moment as we go forth in your Spirit."

DAY 16
NEW NORMAL

*"But he passing through the midst of them went his way,
came down to Capernaum, a city of Galilee, and taught
them on the Sabbath days. And they were astonished at his
doctrine: for his word was with power." (Luke 4:30–32)*

What sets the Word of God apart from all other written works in creation? Why are His words with power? How could Jesus walk right through the middle of a mob of people who hated Him enough to want to stone Him to death right then and there? You want to know this because you want to live within the same kinds of words, with the same back-up, to experience the same results. This is the supernatural "new normal" template for the child of God. It always has been. The supernatural of God is not only a human impossibility; it is God's idea of normal! It stands to reason, then, that we need Him so we can live this way He is.

Holy Spirit delights in creating new normals for you

These are dangerously strong times we're in! We have to believe strong, with a strong word, against a strong enemy, in a strong season. And our God is the All Mighty One. His words as we have them in the Bible, overlook, oversee, and stand forever *over* every other word, every other name, and every other power. All words of God are prophetic in that they speak authoritatively *over the natural.* They are fulfilled in the natural, in their time, and in God's tone.

As living waters continue to wash over you, the truth brings the impurities to the surface. He will speak to you prophetically and bring things up to be processed out. Your "New Normal" will look a whole lot more appealing than the old ways of thinking you used to labor under. But first comes the redirection. Be ready for it. If you hear correction with an attitude of ridicule, cynicism, or deprecation, you can know that this word didn't come forth from the Spirit of Grace. Though He corrects us, and sometimes pointedly, yet He is gentle-hearted and remembers what we are made of: He is a very good Father.

"A Supernatural Redirection." The platform for this correction came as I was studying 1 John. I was in prayer, but not one of much faith, and the Holy Spirit spoke a word of correction to me. Boy, I was embarrassed. I thought I should have been beyond the point of needing this correction. I felt condemned. Right there, I tested it a moment, to discover that the condemnation was coming from *my* heart and not God's. How did I know that? Because from His Word I know He does not *condemn* me and His correction is for my life and well-being.

But He did correct me. And then He asked, "Do you understand Me?" He immediately allowed me to see myself as I responded to Him. In a sudden vision I saw my *bearing* as I was being corrected: I was like a young child who feels ashamed and guilty, my shoulders drooped, my lower lip was in a pout. Because I was embarrassed at having to be reminded of something so elementary, my words came out in a whine. "Yes, Lord," was a thin, self-pitying whisper.

He asked me again, a little stronger, "*Do you understand Me?*" These words coming yet again unnerved me, but I realized I was going to have to give a better answer! I responded again, and my *demeanor* as I received His words *was different this time!* I saw myself deliberately hear, then stand up, square my shoulders, and look straight ahead, a lot more determined, "**Yes**, Lord." This was big (for me)!

But it didn't stop there. *He* was not thinking this was big. The third time, He asked me, "**Do you understand Me!**" He was looking for a much stronger response: **He knew *I* needed something more.** In that moment, I got it. I saw myself stand up boldly with my face set like flint, sparkling eyes, and a firm resolve when I answered with the very same words, but a whole different spirit: "**YES! LORD**!" At that point, you see, it was a done deal. *There was no question **in my mind** that I had gotten this valuable correction into my heart!* And *that* is what God was after."

That response indicates a New Normal. What was *not* normal to me: a bold, demonstrative, faith-filled answer in obedience **became normal for me**! I can't tell you how wonderful it feels to not be fearful. I can't explain what it makes me feel like to know God loves me enough to partake of my life here on earth and love me enough to be a real parent to me.

This New Normal carries over now into everything else I think about. He's dealing with me as a son. We are His children. **He will train us up right, to be upright**. Everything He does in our lives is done out of love because that is who He is. We can rely on His nature to be consistently on our side, for our good. Even when we do wrong, He is not going to thrash us: He will bring redirection and help if we'll seek Him for it.

When a word from the Bible becomes *rhema*—(alive!)—to us, it means that it is prophetically fulfilled then and there, but it may take a long time to see it in the natural. We still know it is done, by faith. It becomes our New Normal. I shared this special visitation in a bad season in my first book. I share it now because after many years, the work it accomplished in my heart has been a finished one ever since that date:

> Aimlessly walking in a grocery store during a harsh and grief-stricken time of life, I was suddenly struck with panic: *what am I going to do! How am I gonna get through this?! I am totally alone!* My knuckles turned white and I was about to faint. Suddenly, I heard the words, **"Fall back . . . into My grace."** The attack stopped *immediately*. It has never happened again. There is now no way I can look at the word *grace* the same way. Grace is a safety net, a strong and cushioned landing place, a strong and gentle saving from death. That word is part of me now. It became prophetic. It still is. What made it prophetic? I heard God say it, and it was real to me! I believed Him and responded to it, trusting in His strength. It came to pass in the next moment.

That was another New Normal. When God helped me, it was a very great help. The result was that I became more set apart to Him, and gladly so. That transformation only began in that moment; every moment since then in this area, my heart is already fixed on God. It was a done deal and continues to be FINISHED." Here's How it Happened:

- I cried out to my Father!
- His powerful words came quickly to save, *Fall Back!*
- If I had any question it would have been, How? Where?
- His prophetic Word came . . . *into My Grace!*
- It was so sudden, so simple and so HIM, *nothing stood in my way* to receive its instant fulfillment

"Now the Lord is that Spirit: and where the Spirit of the Lord is there is liberty. But we all with open face beholding as in a glass the glory of the Lord, are changed into the same image from glory to glory, even as by the Spirit of the Lord." (2 Cor. 3:17, 18)

Holy Spirit provides and uses opportunities to experience and test the veracity of His every Word, and every prophetic word, given by His Spirit

It's a supernatural act of God to create in us a Jesus-filled temperament, a response system of love and faith, truth, strength and gentleness. **Can you imagine how supernaturally it'll touch the world to see us living this way?** He trains us by practice with the goal that we'll be conformed to His image. God is supernaturally molding us through this process of becoming like Him. It brings forth a "response-ability" in which we learn to and *have to* trust Him so He can trust us with more of Him. Again and again, walking on holy ground, His life in us *"becomes us."* This is the prophetic fulfillment of our calling: our New Normal!

It is far less believable to think there is *no* supernatural action going on in us by His Spirit than to believe that there is this very action happening in us *all the time!* You can hear it and see it as you live immersed in Him. It's the outworking of this word from Jesus, "Howbeit when he, the Spirit of truth, is come, he will guide you into all truth: for he shall not speak of himself; but whatsoever he shall hear, *that* shall he speak: and he will shew you things to come. He will glorify Me, for He will take of Mine and will disclose it to you." (John 16:13, 14)

A 24/7 VOICE

"The supernatural of God is not only a human impossibility; it is God's idea of normal!"

Talk to God in your journal. Ask Him to respond and listen. Then write in faith: you know Him and how He is and what His Words sound like in the Bible. Anticipate His present tense voice for a future event that is *just about to happen: your New Normal.*

MANIFEST

"I am ready for a 'new normal' but want it to be Your New Thing in me! Your Holy Spirit's accomplishment, not mine, not my 're-invention' or my own strength. Your Spirit helps me seek and hear You so I can know Your voice, so I can be changed, so You will be glorified in my life."

THE NEXT LEVEL

T he Book of Daniel: his life, ministry, and end-time visions and dreams, all unfolded in spite of great spiritual battle in the heavenlies. Daniel lived in a captive country called Babylon in the Middle East. In fact it was Iraq and Iran *yesterday*, many centuries ago. That same violent spirit still has authority over there. **Yet *Daniel* prevailed**.

On this seventeenth day let's make an attitude shift into *"Overcome."* Let's zoom in on a contrast in scripture that is obvious from the Book of Daniel and throughout the Word: there are victors and there are victims:

1. First, "I beheld, and the same horn *made war with the saints and prevailed against them.*" (Dan. 7:21)
2. Second, "But the *people that do know their God shall be strong and do exploits.*" (Dan. 32b)

It is possible that in the very same world with the very same enemy, in the very same locale, believers can be both prevailed upon and killed, and also know their God so well that they are strong and do exploits. What we may not be so sure about is **whether you and I have a lot to say about which group we will be in**. I believe we do.

Many people do not have that choice for one reason or another. I'm thinking of new believers in Iraq and Iran, in fact, who have no access to the Word except for a page ripped from a Bible somewhere else and smuggled into their hands. Maybe all they had was a *dream* in which they saw Jesus!

Without having learned from God's own words that believers are called to exercise a great gift of faith, so much so that miracles are the order of the day, the enemy has an advantage over believers.

They might not find out that they are more than conquerors through Christ; that believers have authority over principalities and powers through Jesus Christ and in the power of the *Name* of Jesus; and that He will guide, protect, answer, and provide. Many of us have lived some of our time without this powerfully prophetic Word ourselves, so we have an idea how limited this kind of faith-life is.

Even if the enemy kills us, does he have the *final victory*? No. The saints beheaded for the name of Christ have a seat as close to God as possible. They are precious to Him. Either way, in Christ we overcome. **But you and I have a choice to make about how we respond to adversity and to His Word.** What we see as a stark contrast in the Daniel verses about life outcomes has a lot to do with how *we* respond when we enter trials. To get through the coming darkness and shine brighter than ever, we will have to know our God. We're called to answer in the next level, and much of that next level is entered by faith with eyes and ears open to His 24/7 Voice. Imagine getting so determined in our hearts that who He says we are *is who we are*, that we will cry out for it over all else; demand it, declare it; grab hold and not let go! That is the Next Level.

> *Around the world, in every venue and time zone, day or night,*
> *in any season, in persecution or provision, in every language,*
> *natural or spiritual, there is a 24/7 Voice we can hear*

We're talking about a feast we don't always partake of, yet it's there all the time. If you are bored with life in Christ it could be because you're living in the analysis mode of an unbeliever. Make your analysis in terms of what **Jesus** said life in Him was like. Be ready to make a break with decorum and proper living in the world . . . and in some parts of the Church, too.

We don't have to belly up to a table that offers a version of Buffet-Bible. We don't have to pattern ourselves after the world to win anyone. We do not have to bow to an angry special interest group when it is God's Word on the line. Someone has to tell people they aren't God. And we'd better know that ourselves, first. Let's dine with the Lord Himself, feasting on His living words while He works.

When it's our turn for Bibles to be outlawed or taken away, there should still be an indelible word making its mark in our hearts. God has a word that is constantly illustrating itself to us in prophetic ways, if we have eyes to see and ears to hear. That 24/7 Voice is God's Word made alive in and through His creation, flowing into the living waters He pours into our hearts.

A powerful shift has already begun in the last several years. The season of the supernatural has begun to exhibit in our natural life-style, changing longtime situations and circumstances, relationships and people. It's like the Father is pushing things around in heaven, like I used to move the furniture in my bedroom. Something new is to come from this season as the world caves in. Something good. **We will not cave in!** He's showing us how we can thrive in spirit, in spite of everything going on around us. And He's showing us He can answer prayer offered up for decades.

The Lord gave me counsel I needed one night. He spoke as if I was sitting right across Him, spoke directly to me.

"5 Reasons You Should Never Look Back"

1. You mean you gave your life to the Master and you'd consider giving up that ground you've already taken? The ground you already fought and nearly died for to make it this far? Listen, we're in this together!
2. Maybe you think it's easier to walk backward to avoid facing your trouble? Try it. You think you're fainting from the battle now: try back-tracking away from the ground you've taken, into a potential death trap because now you didn't see it.
3. You are safe on the ground I have chosen for you, child. You always suspected it wouldn't be easy. (And as I heard Ken Copeland's voice say) "I didn't tell you about the giants because to me they aren't giants." Now let's use these difficulties for life and not for death. See beyond your situation: are you really willing to *disobey*?
4. Weary? Afraid? Losing hope? I'm not. So why not fall back into My grace? Falling back into old habits and patterns that didn't work are far too confining for the expansion of your spirit I'm working on.
5. You should never look back because it's the **wrong direction!** My soul would be very sad if you gave up.

God's invitation to His people: *Come to the Next Level*! It's not only imperative we know how to discern and walk out visions that come to us—it is also unbelievably exciting! It's what the church has gone without for far too long, under the guise of checking that our faith isn't built on emotion. These days He is redeeming the time to get us ready for what comes next—the glorious fulfillment of every *jot* and *tittle* of scripture from start to finish! His return will be the crowning touch. I don't know about you, but wherever I am, I plan on being very emotional about that event.

"Ye have not chosen me, but I have chosen you, and ordained you, that ye should go and bring forth fruit, and that your fruit should remain: that whatsoever ye shall ask of the Father in my name, he may give it you. These things I command you, that ye love one another." (John 15:16, 17)

Let's go further into what this "next level" looks like. Consider that this is the very way we are to be able to love our enemies. It's easy to love friends. But another *next level* is enemy territory. There we are also called to love. But not just called: commanded. There is a deeper meaning to all things prophetic: it is for God to reach the world.

A 24/7 VOICE

"When our Bibles are outlawed or taken away, there should still be **an indelible word making its mark in our hearts**. He has a **word that is constantly illustrating itself to us** in prophetic ways, if we have eyes to see and ears to hear." Now believe it, recall, and write. Your ears are open, so hear what God just said to you in these comments. Remember His loving kindness to you. Maybe a picture somewhere comes to mind. I'm seeing a shield . . . but is it protecting me from an evil, or am I using it to shield myself from the power of God to change me? Are you praying in the Spirit when you hear something compelling?

MANIFEST

"The next level is where I have to be, God, closer to You, readier for what comes; able to rise above anything, with and in Your provision. How else

can I reach into anyone else's life with equipping or activation in what they need? Move in power in my life, I give you permission again."

DAY 18
PROPHETIC FLOW

This *practical, powerful, prophetic!* Let's look at how the life of Jesus looks and sounds as it flows in us to reveal God's plans and purposes in these days.

> The flow of the Holy Spirit is like living waters coming down from the mountain of God, making its way into valleys of shadows to bring forth cleansing and healing. It's rivers charging over mountain cliffs and waterfalls that drench the earth as they continue to the sea. The flow of the Holy Spirit is like ocean waves surging upward to plunge down into other waves, into other depths of water, to take authority over and bring out the old and exchange for the new. Holy Spirit has tides of living water, carrying in refreshment and power, and going out, carrying out debris and dirt. Living waters are alive with God.

The closest likeness to water that I am aware of is words. When He spoke to Isaiah, it sounded like His words to and through Isaiah; when He spoke to Ezekiel, it sounded like the Truth coming through Ezekiel. John the Baptist was, whew! . . . John the Baptist. All, amazing. But let's tune in to a different response to prophetic flow from one who also went through the waters, so to speak.

When The Spirit spoke to Jonah, though . . . Jonah was scared to death to obey. The Lord's voice was diminished and he reacted in his own strength to avoid "the sound" of heaven! For Jonah, repentance by Nineveh was so outrageous it was not to be believed. That being his problem, he thought it all out rationally and came to the wrong conclusions. He probably was afraid that if they deserved death, which they did, and his words predicted destruction, which they deserved, then if they did repent and destruction was averted, there would be plenty of ruthless people who never believed *any* of it who would want to kill him because he tried to manipulate repentance; they would deduce he was a charlatan.

To Jonah, all this felt like the weight of the world on him. It *was* the weight of the world! He didn't see it as the sound of *heaven*. The pressure was too great! The situation was too big, too scary, too much like his own death sentence. But, it was his own disobedience to the voice of the Lord that almost killed him. God had to show him what real pressure was, deep down and under the ocean. Eventually, when he repented (changed his mind), he heard. It should encourage you that even if you were swallowed by adversity, you will still hear God's voice if you turn your ear to hear (respond to, turn to) Him.

Resistance to the Word stops the flow of God's purposes

When someone hears God's Word and has a bad reaction to it, it's either because it has shown them their source of pain, or it's a prophetic word that goes deeper than they see and hear yet. If you can prophetically flow into this breach with living waters, God can lift them to their next level, closer to faith. Thank God, that voice is constantly speaking; the Spirit is always ready to speak a word in all hearts.

You can hear the sounds of heaven. They are the stirring in your heart to rise up and believe what God said is happening today! Prophetic flow is tuning in, jumping in, immersing your heart in the Holy Spirit's constant speaking, wooing, directing, nudging, encouraging, and ministering Spirit. In prophetic flow, worship is the door. Praying in the Holy Ghost are the steps inside. That which is prophetic is the fragrance, the air, the atmosphere, once inside. We can live, move, and have our being in the flow of words of life to us from God's throne.

When I provide examples or excerpts from prophetic words given to me, I'm hoping it is like priming a water pump. Hopefully you will feel a rising up of God's own voice in you. I hope you start to remember prophetic words from your experience. My experiences are small compared to others. That is why God can use them to speak to a great many people who think they just can't live this way, when in fact that is not true. Your life is made of experiences. Faith produces experiences. *Experience* is not a bad word. We are in *relationship* with Holy Spirit, and relationship engenders experience (If it doesn't, you have to wonder what kind of relationship it really is).

Each prophet, each believer, has a language with God that is unique to them, to fulfill the purpose of God through them. The Lord directed this book to help *you* see and hear Jesus spiritually, in the language you and He have together. It is truly a love language, and becomes stronger as a result of obedience, with time and in faith. One time in prayer and while journaling, the Lord reminded me:

> "I AM (is) in control of your children's futures and you do not need to keep reminding Me of My job: *when* to save and deliver. You keep bringing up things you have already prayed about and given to Me. Don't you believe I heard you? Or do you doubt that I will help you after I did hear? Either way, you are calling My character into question." I kept missing His voice as He tried to re-encourage me, because fear was clinging to me! I kept voicing my own fear, hearing my own voice over His Word. Finally He spoke yet once more, stern-ly, "**I *SAID*, Your children belong to Me: *Do you hear me*?!**"

Yikes. Yes, I heard Him that time. I repented and took hold of peace with a new strength in my fingertips . . . it was something more like *a new grasp*. It began a prophetic flow over the months in which I received healing for much grief.

That's what happened to the people of God in the Bible who heard from Him in their hearts and then were moved upon to respond to Him in a specific way. Most of the Word of God is the result of super-natural interactions with God. It happened as they walked with God and got to know His voice better, trust Him more, and respond more personally.

The prophetic manifests itself in faith mixed with action: God's and ours. Remember, they didn't even have the written word like we do. . . and yet,

- Noah was instructed to build an ark for an event he'd never seen: Rain. Flood.
- Abraham saw up to the stars and down to the sand and was given a promise

- Joseph dreamed dreams that directed his life and saved nations
- Moses was guided into all the details of the earthly Tabernacle so it would be just like the Heavenly one
- Deborah was given wisdom how to act boldly to bring deliverance to Israel
- Jeremiah was instructed to "see" differently, God explained what it all meant, he spoke prophetically, and it happened
- David wrote music prophetically through acrostic psalms
- Elijah worked miracles when he heard and obeyed what God told him to do
- Daniel watched God shut the mouths of hungry lions
- Joseph was warned in a dream to take Mary and flee to Egypt
- Peter saw a vision that opened the door to his heart—and into reality—for the Gentiles
- Paul was delivered time after time when angry crowds tried to corner him or kill him
- And then there's The Revelation of John

It's time to believe. Not just for you and yours. It's time for the *nations* to turn, whosoever will, and be carried into the flow of the Spirit for His soon return. We're in a season gearing up for the return of our King and the ushering in of the Kingdom where, "They shall not hurt nor destroy in all My holy mountain, for the earth shall be full of the knowledge of the LORD as the waters cover the sea. And in that day there shall be a Root of Jesse, Who shall stand as a banner to the people; for the Gentiles shall seek Him, and His resting place shall be glorious." (Is. 11:9, 10)

Now *that* is prophetic flow.

A 24/7 VOICE

It rained for forty days, you know, and all life ceased except for what was in the ark. The prophetic flow of God had spoken far earlier when He said, *Repent, people, from what's killing you (sin), or it'll kill you!* They resisted this arresting announcement. "Resistance to the Word will stop the prophetic flow . . ." Can you see a picture of this?

No? Well, get out your crayons and make one. Glue words that mean something to you in the water you draw.

MANIFEST

"I know and flow with You, Holy Spirit, because I am in You and allow Your movement in my life. You speak through me and I flow with your words. I declare there will be nothing standing in the way of Your prophetic flow. You are doing this kind of thing in these last days."

DAY 19
WHEN GOD WANTS TO TALK

"And thine ears shall hear a word behind thee, saying,
This is the way, walk ye in it, when ye turn to the right
hand, and when ye turn to the left." (Is. 30:21)

C an you tell, as you deliberately draw closer to God in these weeks, you're heading in to a deeper place where God speaks more clearly? Where you can see His picture a lot clearer? We have important provision (*pro-vision*) for what happens next in life. Holy Spirit can speak them in prayer time, from the Word, in visions and dreams. When they come to us they are gifts, with four intentions from the Holy Spirit:

- He wants our undivided attention—with no distractions
- He provides loving, practical instruction for the needs we'll encounter
- He adds a bit of prophetic surprise, the personal God-sign that it was He who thought it up
- He follows His words with circumstances that require, confirm, and fulfill what those words fore-told

We are not trusting just *any* supernatural! We are trusting Jehovah-God, and trusting His Word. Jesus went to the cross, not simply as a human rights action. He did that for every individual ever to come into and exit this world. The cross is a deeply personal action. It is a one-to-one invitation and divine intervention. Because of the cross, when God wants to talk we're invited to a 24/7 Word-Feast.

When God wants to talk, it's going to be prophetic!
It's going to accomplish what He sent it to do!

Isaiah prophesied God's heart: "So shall my word be that goes forth from my mouth: it shall not return unto me void, but it shall accomplish that which I please, and it shall prosper in the thing whereto I sent it." (Is. 55:11) I like to remind myself that the next verse is what this strong promise will accomplish in us: "For you shall go out with joy, and be led forth with peace." (vs. 12)

Nineteen days into this practical, powerful, prophetic "fast," if you want to hear God better: come up higher; go deeper. Here's a secret for success: do not evade the hard situations you're in. Don't run from them or confess them into mere pit-stops along the way. Address them as a king or a priest would! **When God wants to speak** it is to instill something in us we didn't have before that conversation. Things like teach-ability. Authority. Perseverance. Love. Strategies. Victory. And of course, patience. Every single day is an invitation to hear when God wants to talk.

In 2010 God made some huge changes in my life. **They were initiated and accomplished through Holy Spirit's prophetic interchanges.** It began with a supernatural download of Holy Spirit's intentions for me. Here's how it happened.

> In 2007 I was in Florida as my step mother was dying of cancer. My father was at her bedside day and night, just as he had been at the bedside of my own mother twenty years prior as she lay dying of cancer. He was exhausted, broken hearted, and silent. I was walking toward the bedroom where I saw him sitting, dozing, his head against the bedrail of the hospital bed, when **I heard these words clearly in my spirit**: "That man is not going to be alone when it is his time to go." I knew in that moment Holy Spirit had commissioned *me* to go. This was no one else's but *my* assignment, for He had told *me*.

Now, can I just tell you something? This is not what I would have chosen to do. But I have been saved from many situations in my life with Jesus, so I trusted Him on this one: my Dad was worth it. It was several years before it came to pass. I waited on the Lord for timing, and it was very obvious when it became time, for I was finally able to accept this change. I didn't want to leave my family, friends of forty years, and the comfort of my own 'hood. I didn't want to begin again from nothing at my age. But I said yes to God, to obey. I give Him the glory for it. *As a sign to me*, He literally arranged every detail, start to finish, including loading a moving van that costed me almost nothing, getting my two cats to Florida without my driving them there (that was worth a lot, and almost miraculous when you think about it), and many more unusual helps. I arrived and settled in. This began the best new season I have ever experienced!

In other words, His word, whether prophetically spoken or in The Book, sets us in place: at the right time, in the right place, with perfect provision. **His words are fulfilling themselves in us.** Can I tell you how prophetic those words were to me? It was from this place of re-assignment, with everything new and to be learned and discovered, that many of the fulfillments of my entire life have begun springing forth. Why here? Why now? Why not there? Why not then? God knows. It was a risk. It was not what I would have thought up to do with my life. I had no idea what I was doing, I just knew **it was for me to obey.** I'm thankful for the grace He gave me to hear Him speak this word in my heart and then move on it.

I awoke one morning and had a vision. When I saw it, I knew it was me it was referring to because there was a little art project going on in it. It had lots of color, too. It was like this:

> I saw a tiny figure from behind. She was putting together an art project, a mosaic overlay on a concrete bird bath. She was working on making a fountain. Chip by chip, she glued on one after another in a colorful pattern she had in her mind. All of a sudden, my vision panned out! I see (it's still present tense to me!) **a huge gusher of water fly out** of that fountain; such a huge explosion of water that it flew off the sides of my vision, if you can imagine that! Then I heard the words, as from One grinning, Now ***THAT's* a** FOUNTAIN.

I believe *when God wants to talk,* He can circumvent our own beliefs, strengths or intellect by speaking in dreams, words, and visions. A lot of other people believe it these days, too! This is how countless people groups have been reached over centuries by Jesus. Muslims are having visions of the Lord Jesus. Nation and people groups who never heard of Jesus are hearing from Him! **This is how your sons** and daughters will be reached when you can't reach them with what *you* think are the words they need to hear.

A 24/7 VOICE

When God wants to talk, He can speak anywhere: are you ready? Can you recall a dream you had in which you were aware it had a deeper meaning? Include as many details as possible. Remember the basic rule of engagement with Holy Spirit: scripturally accurate. If you are dreaming regularly, it's probably time for a separate **dream journal** in addition to your regular journal. Get used to writing His explanations and instructions in your journals, as well as how words, dreams and visions made you feel. If it's all in a journal or two, you'll always have them in place to recall.

MANIFEST

"You speak, and miracles are about to spring forth! When I hear Your words and believe them, they become prophetic to me. I receive wisdom in the night. My ears listen and my eyes are on You. Brain, be still and know He is God, and not you."

DAY 20
IN YOUR DREAMS

The next two days will finish our journey in Living Words, Prophetic and Powerful, and prepare for a Prophetic Shift you've been looking forward to. Today, in your dreams, we're going to discover more about a powerful way God has spoken through the centuries. It's my favorite way, and I can't help but think it's one of God's faves, also. It's because I can't try to out-think or out-talk Him while He's speaking.

You just can't ignore them, but you can't quite remember them. They appear and entertain you, trouble you, look crazy, and mean *something*, but what?! Our dreams are valuable real estate to God, who sometimes may have no alternative but to contact you in your dreams.

For anyone who says, "I don't dream," it simply means they don't recall dreaming. Dreaming *automatically* happens when *anyone* sleeps, according to decades of research, and probably a lot more often each night in our sleep cycles than any of us are aware. Think about this: Babies dream, animals dream, so do people who can't *see* in the natural (they're blind). Tell me, what can babies be dreaming about? I think they dream about heaven, though I have no proof. I know you've seen dogs sound asleep on their sides, with their legs running and their mouths muffling out barks!

The night itself is a priceless parcel of time *for the Holy Spirit*, as our sleep accounts for at least one third of our lives. At the same time, and I am sure this must be a "coincidence," many people find it an unsettling time. You're laying there in your bed, *thinking* when you should be drifting off to sleep. It's dark out. And you're thinking too much. You could even call it worrying. In the dark. The alarm clock is ticking next to your ear. And it's *late*. It's too quiet. Your shirt is itchy.

It's *really dark*. Is that a noise you heard in the hallway? The fan is wobbling. You blow your nose. Look at the clock. Now it's even later! As you probably suspect, here in the night watches, there is also a battle going on to *hold* this piece of dream-time real estate. If you've done your spiritual warfare before you get in bed, you can rest much better in the night season. (Ps. 3:5; 4:8)

When your eyes close and you fall asleep, the next phases of sleep are comprised of rest **and reflection**. That much has been verified by scientific experimentation and observation. Scientists can explain a hundred aspects of this phenomenon called sleep, and I'm sure there is accuracy along with much to be learned. But from science and from the Lord we can understand this much: *Everyone* dreams, and God is no respecter of persons. That's the most important part. If you want to dissect it every way from Sunday, just don't excise the part that lets you know how spiritually beneficial it is.

When we sleep, the world is not in charge. We are not in charge. This is God's time with us. He is in charge. Our spirit stays awake. He meets with us there often. Imagine that, God is looking forward to an evening speaking with us while *we* listen, *because* we are asleep.

I believe dreaming is in some ways like how the writers of the inspired Word of God received and wrote their messages. Not that they slept (though they could have: what difference does it make?), but that they had allowed Holy Spirit to take the lead as they listened. Embedded in scripture, we find verses inserted in the flow of verses that seem disjointed from the main theme. Then, after a long time they suddenly present as fulfilled prophecy on a date much later. We may think logically when we are awake, but when the lights go out and our brain snoozes, the spirit does not think analytically like we think it should think! God is more *calculated* than that.

Rather, the creative side takes over with a flourish! Our dreams pull together a modernist re-mix that includes items of the day, symbols, people we do and don't know who may or may not represent others; we see colors and trees, words floating and water we can swim under while breathing. There are flying things and sometimes they are *us*. Animals talk with us and we walk with them as friends. Roads may turn into steep cliffs and trouble our spirits. These details usually have a purpose in a dream to instruct us.

It's a wondrous thing to hear from the God of the Bible even when we're asleep—our own strength and talents don't even come into play or get in the way of His communication. Holy Spirit dreams, visions, and words give us applicable glimpses into the eternal normal.

4 Provisions from Prophetic Dreaming

1. comfort and encouragement
2. illustration that will direct our lives
3. an alarm that shows us something important we must know
4. clues to how to walk out our assignment and mission

A dream I had in 2012 provided all four of these helps.

> I was feeding a fat baby, so gorged its eyes were glazed. The baby's mouth took it in but then it oozed back out. The food couldn't go down. *Nothing was really reaching him.* I picked him up and realized that he only had a head. His "body" *was a work glove.* The glove was bloated, filthy, heavy and saturated like a soggy diaper. There was a man in front of me. I gave the baby to the man, whom I was now following out of the room, and then went into another room and found a clean one-sy for the baby. I laid it out on the bed; it was a light green; it was the accurate shape of a baby body, but with no baby in it.

I prayed about the dream and received these explanations. The baby is the church that is still not awake and actively growing strong. It's over-fed and kept drowsy and inactive with too much *food* (instruction without living it). The body shape of a misshapen soggy work glove indicated that its works had not changed to produce a young child with no need of diapers. Now the glove was completely filled out with what needed to be *cleaned* out. Is it possible that somewhere the body had decided that eating was its work? *Who taught him that?* He was taking in food (knowledge) but never working with it, never working it out into his growth and place in the world. His faith had turned to consumption, or "the act of consuming, as by *use, decay, or destruction.*" (Webster's) That man was the Lord Jesus. He took charge when in the course of time there was intercession for the church.

The act of laying out a little outfit for the cleaned baby to be put into suggested that the baby would again come into a healthy, clean, nourished, but not gluttonous new life. The baby's new outfit was *green*: signifying a lively hope. There would be a Jesus-ordained change here, in that He changed the "soggy diaper work glove" for a clean one piece (unity of the Spirit) outfit.

You will eventually be the best person to interpret your dreams as you learn God's special way of communicating with you. Praying in the Spirit, communing with the Lord, ingesting the Word, with obedience following, is the recipe for that language. There's an abundance of word meanings in scripture: numbers have meanings, trees have significance, the phrase *many waters*, leviathan, the colors, and hundreds more objects help you recognize what may be happening in your dreams, and even what you see while awake.

For example, regarding learning your personal prophetic language with Holy Spirit, I want to point out something about the color green here in this dream. It's worth noting that many people identify the color green in dreams as referring to jealousy, envy, or even death (like the color of the *pale* horse in Rev. 6:8). But for me personally, this color has always represented hope. In the Bible, green also represents *luxuriant life*, as in trees and plants. The Hebrew word for green is *raanan, flourishing*: (Psalm 52:8) "I am like a green olive tree in the house of the Lord." Do the work to learn how the Spirit of God communicates with you personally. Books can be very helpful but you will have your own way of seeing things, also. APPENDIX D has sources that may help.

God knows all our dreams and may or may not need for us to know what they mean. I've had dreams I did remember that I never could figure out. Other times I've had dreams I couldn't remember that I felt were immensely important. I'm saying this to encourage you to expect dreams, expect interpretations. Expect dreams to be a strong part of the deep relationship that is special to you and God. Expect, also, to not remember some of them. In due season *you'll get comfortable seeing and hearing in this way*. "In a dream, in a vision of the night, when deep sleep falleth upon men, in slumberings upon the bed; when deep sleep falleth upon men, then he openeth the ears of men, and sealeth their instruction" (Job 33:15–17)

A 24/7 VOICE

Revelation does not come *from* our brains, but it eventually *reaches* our brains. Open your Concordance and search out what the Bible has to say about **dreams, sleep, and rest**: where they come from, why they are important, how God feels about your sleeping in the night, and all the things God has done historically in those avenues of communication. **This information will become part of your prophetic language with Holy Spirit.** I can just about guarantee you'll know a lot more about *your* dreams when the Word has informed you of the basics. Write down those dreams you remember, *whether you can understand them or not.* Write down how they make you feel. You can go back later and recall with more understanding as you get it.

MANIFEST

"Our God gives instruction and direction in our night hours. I am serious about hearing, seeing, remembering, processing, and receiving wisdom in them! My being awake or asleep doesn't limit You from speaking; but my willingness to hear You does. I declare that as You instruct me, I learn and grow so I can be who You've called me to be."

DAY 21
JOURNAL, SONG AND PSALM

"But as it is written, Eye hath not seen, nor ear heard, neither have entered into the heart of man, the things which God hath prepared for them that love him. But God hath revealed them unto us by his Spirit: for the Spirit searcheth all things, yea, the deep things of God. For what man knoweth the things of a man, save the spirit of man which is in him? Even so the things of God knoweth no man, but the Spirit of God. Now we have received, not the spirit of the world, but the spirit which is of God; that we might know the things that are freely given to us of God." (1 Cor. 2:9–12)

Every creative act a person does or makes is prophetic. When David wrote his psalms, *they were prayers, songs, or writings. They were not scripture at that time. But they are* now. They were prophetic words. One of the indicators of godly prophetic writing is that Jesus Christ is lifted up; our sites become set on God's salvation, faith is strengthened, and God gets great glory. Plenty of times, David was overwhelmed by trouble. He just didn't leave it there. He took his burdens to God and set a new tone for his thoughts to begin a new song.

Journaling is a form of communicating with God; it's meditating on a word or theme He is inspiring you to search out from the scriptures, and writing what you're gleaning. In the process of listening and chronicling, God's voice gets clearer, a bit here, and more there. You come to new conclusions, you get built up and encouraged. **You recognize His voice.**

Journaling provides us with a place to enter our scheduled and surprise meetings with Holy Spirit. This is part of your history in the making. God reveals things to us that convince us that He is real and present with us. We write them down. From there, who knows what can come of them, but at least they are out from inside you where they can only help you. What if God's plan is to use you to reach many people with the revelation He is opening to you!

When Holy Spirit directs them to someone else, these words convince *them* that God is who He says He is because *only God knew that information!* It gives *them* a faith they never had before. And now, the invitation is out there for them to respond. It's good to remember that wisdom is not just to be held in and acted on, it is to be shared so others can live, too. Put to anointed and inspired music, those words become prophetic to others as they wash into the atmosphere.

We are a people of hearing and receptivity. Listening to the sounds of heaven changes the way we hear earth

I had been listening to some amazing instrumental worship music when I suddenly realized I was receiving a spiritual download. I quickly grabbed my pen and pad so I could capture it on paper. Too many treasures get lost to time and generations because we put off an immediate response. If we realized how important those moments of revelation are, we would recognize our procrastination by its other name, disobedience.

I had to say, Ouch, when I journaled this. Maybe you need it like I do.

This territory of the prophetic, strangely, has been hidden in full view. It's been waiting to be discovered in these last times before we see Him face to face. When the Spirit calls us to come up *now*, he means in the spirit, not at some unforeseen catching-away-moment in the future. Our intimate times with God in worship are "practice" for being in close communion with Him at all future times. What glorious practice.

If scientists have found new dimensions of outer space that astound us . . . if molecular biologists have discovered smaller worlds of matter than anyone ever dreamed of . . . why should we doubt for one second that we can enter deeper, unimagined dimensions of God's Kingdom coming in these days before heaven touches earth? In plain sight, His own Word says He wants us to see and know: "While we look not at the things which are seen, but at the

things which are not seen: for the things which are seen are temporal; but the things which are not seen are eternal." (2 Cor. 4:18)

So, let's go back here for a moment. When I don't respond quickly
enough to write it down when I get a word, I begin to hear *another*
voice whispering: "Aw, *that* is not any profound thing! It's hardly
worth your time to turn on the light and open that journal." Or, another whisper seeps in with, "Who do you think you are, thinking
you have anything of importance to think on! Anyway, everyone
knows *that!*" Someone was trying to keep that valuable piece of revelation from seeing the light of day! That's why obedience is a **now**
thing. Settle it in your mind that you just might be hungry enough to
hear from Holy Spirit that it is worth the sacrifice. Tell your flesh to
read 1 Samuel 15:22 . . . but have your spirit hear it. I'm only telling
you what I tell myself. Our time to come up closer, go higher and yet
deeper, is for *this* season when we need it before He returns.

Prayer, music and worship, journaling under the influence of the
Spirit of God all bring words of wisdom and comfort to the light of
day. What starts as prayer and fellowship turns easily to worship and
creative prophetic interchanges. Here are five ways to approach personal and journaling time that can flow into songs and worship:

- **Here's my problem, Lord.** Get the ingredients of it together:
  state it and put it into the pot to simmer: cast the care of it on
  the Lord (1 Pet. 5:7). Then "put it on the stove," or, seek the
  Lord and His Word for your need/desire or solution. Do not
  dwell on your problem. Your goal is to hear from God and
  come to solutions

- **I'm available Lord.** When we belong to God, we have a
  potentially unlimited opportunity for meeting. Your time
  with Him as you watch and listen expectantly opens the door
  of His strategies. (Hab. 2:1)

- **Here are my dreams, Lord.** Just because you have dreams
  it doesn't mean they are not God's dreams for you! He will
  clarify everything. This is your blessing: to come to know
  Him better because you *have* to (Prov. 25:2)

- **I need to see something new, Lord.** It may be a new
  perspective, a correction, or something new from something

"old" or familiar. In these days so much is being revealed to turn over the tables of old and tired relationship with Father. He's growing our hunger level for His voice. He's leading us to glean something spiritual from something ordinary, all the time and everywhere. (Jer. 1:11)

- **What do You think about that, Lord?** When life has turned an unexpected corner, ask your Lord about it and then let Him talk. The more you ask about, the more you get answers for, seen from His Word's perspective and revealed in intimate times with God (Jer. 33:3)

Your headway into the prophetic will blossom when you talk to God and hear back, when you can look around you and discern valuable ideas from God from simple things around you. **Your prophetic journaling is part of anointed prayer, worship, and study time.** Many "suddenlies" come through intimate time with Him. Many songs that literally turn over the tables of someone's life can come from your worship, songs, and journaling.

I will grow you up into full authority of sonship in this season. It's **still a growing season** . . . it's not drought, not famine . . . not for *you*. I AM perfecting that which concerns you and that means **a time of flourishing and newness**. There is **a season of harvest** coming that you have not even thought of, things you will reap from countless seeds you've sown in faith. As you listen with spiritual ears, receive what I tell you by faith, for I give good advice and have the discernment you need.

I will impart a determination and desperation for Me that makes demands in the spiritual world. **Ask Me for the Spirit of "revolutionary revelation"! Exercise your faith and you will know My Word better as a result.** The season of drought and famine of the Word *is* on its way, but not for you. My intention for you is for My anointing to pour forth, no longer just in you, but *from* you, in song and in many and varied creative actions that speak of Me. It's your heritage that *we* rule and reign together, so press into this season of creativity and worship. **Listen for, seek, and expect Me**; for when I do this thing in you, when it happens, it will seem like it happened suddenly. But we both remember it has been a long process for the seeds to spring to life. It is still a growing season, and it shall continue to be!

A 24/7 VOICE

Writing your account of how the Lord is cleaning out the debris lodged in your mind is part of your spiritual story. It's a process of time, of weeding out, and what has happened in the pressure wash phase. People need to hear our stories, *our* supernatural encounter and prophetic life with God. As a believer in Christ Jesus, **God has told you things. He has shown you things that can speak to others.** You can help people realize there's a God who is big enough to hear *them*, reach *them*, change *them*, and *love them* without measure. "My heart is indicting a good matter: I speak of the things which I have made touching the king: my tongue is the pen of a ready writer." (Psalm 45:1)

MANIFEST

"LORD, You are the caller, the perfecter, the Speaker in this house. You have gifts: songs, words, heart attitudes that need to be shared. What You give me I will share and not hold back. I am ready to get on with Your work: help me go deeper in You."

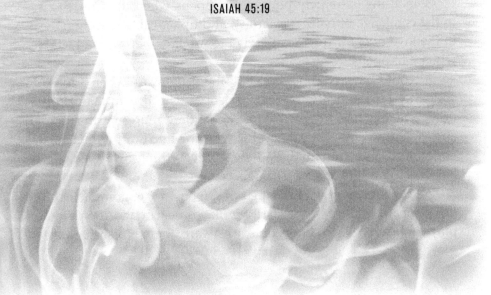

PART 4

LOOKING TO HEAVEN

PROPHETIC SHIFT

"I have not spoken in secret, from somewhere in a land of darkness; I have not said to Jacob's descendants, 'Seek me in vain.' I, the LORD, speak the truth; I declare what is right."

ISAIAH 45:19

DAY 22
PRIORITY

was hastily getting ready for a meeting. As I was brushing my teeth and preparing to go,

> I suddenly saw a crushing and crashing of tectonic plates in front of me. The land, a great section of it, went down from the east heading west, while the other side, the left side went up and over! It put the nation in a tumult. But the people of God were *on high ground, having been in place before the fact.* They had a perspective of *overlooking* because they were prepared beforehand. Their message became hearable and welcomed by many. They lost much also, they sustained damage, but the more important part was that, "in this catastrophic time, the Church will rise and go over. In supernatural inner and outer strength, they will benefit from My Presence in them in this trouble, having opportunity to touch hearts with what is coming **by the sudden shift in priorities."**

Something extremely powerful happens when the Church rises to the challenge of nature, calamity, and upheaval, and dominates it in the love of God. Today is the day to prepare: **before the fact**. Not when it happens.

It would be easy enough to be caught unaware when a tornado suddenly blows in. I know many people who dream about tornadoes, and I've had my own. Most agree they represent the sudden and violent storms of life that come whirling into our perimeters, unannounced and uninvited, and sweep everything away leaving us helpless to protect or save a thing.

As we begin Part 4, "Looking to Heaven," we're going to explore this delicate balance of the part we play on earth and the part God plays in heaven. As many people are aware, there is a shift going on to prepare the saints for something coming. Not only is heaven coming closer to earth by God's great provision but earth is crying out for heaven to come to us! (Rom. 8:19) So let's talk a little about this growing shift in our priorities, for that will be how God gathers us closer, and then, up. The coming calamities are not something to look forward to, exactly. What will the appearance of end time events on earth do to how we look at life, at our desires; at our relationships, and especially at God? How can we be sure we will stand? **This is about priority.** This is about being prepared *before* the *fact*, before *anything* happens.

There are videoed accounts of tornadoes coming directly at a group of believing Christians who prayed and *shouted aloud to the tornado, to get out of here, turn aside!* **And it did.** In the mighty Name of Jesus, it did. They were experiencing the supernatural in a time of sudden need, with God very present and His Words triggering in them the response they needed to save lives. Here's an important part of their faith: **It didn't seem logical; it didn't sound reasonable; they responded in faith which might have felt inadequate or woefully pitiful! They obeyed His Word! In the tempest the very forces of nature at their worst were told what they had to do.** This was a miracle of course. This went against the human response action of fear. Judgment and mercy work together in God's commodities because He wants us all to reach, seek, and find Him.

Many believers insist that God sends judgment on a nation that has fallen away. Many more believe that since Jesus shed His blood to be the propitiation for sin, God would not send judgment on a nation. No one is taking into account that if a nation writes God out of their history, shuts Him out of their laws, out of their classrooms and substitutes it with every conceivable disgrace, filth, murder of innocents, and so on . . . *that nation has of their own accord put themselves in good standing with the prince of darkness who will see to it that that this nation is destroyed,* if he can. Our work, our territory, mission field, and priority in coming days is to alert people to turn to the Lord for salvation and deliverance.

God in His mercy will step back **at a nation's insistence** and allow the level of trouble it will take **to awaken people** to righteousness. For the believer, we have to be ready with a faith filled heart so we don't get dragged into fear, fury or rebellion. We must see with His eyes and hear with ears . . . like animals seem to have when a tsunami is on its way across an ocean, coming toward them. Long before a human being has a clue, the animals are gathering their own and heading for higher ground away from the water.

We are the people of God who hear the voice of God in the maelstrom

Watch and pray, and hear in the spirit of your mind when you see troubles coming a long way off. Like a watchman on the wall, be ready to sound the alarm even if it isn't welcomed as good news. Be available to give an answer for the peace and hope you exhibit. We have the words of life. (1 Pet. 3:15) Hearing and seeing prophetically and obeying the voice of the Lord in the hour of duress will save lives and impact eternities. We can start today by humbling our hearts to learn His ways and hear His words.

Throughout the Old Testament, God sent judgment to save His people from spiritual, moral *extinction*. It's what the world today identifies as the actions of a malicious, hateful God. **They don't understand what God knows about how sin kills people.**

Many people are preparing for disastrous times with food, water, guns, and so on. Others say, how long do 200 MREs last . . . especially if your neighbors come hunting them down and you're standing in the way? Even if you get to eat all those meals, then what? You die anyway? This is not my place to speak to these things, but it is my place here to suggest that **walking with your eyes and ears open will be as necessary and in demand as clean water.** Holy Spirit can direct you to uncontaminated water; He can clean the contaminated water; He can bring new water forth from heaven; He can have you speak to a rock to give it. **The time to turn our eyes toward heaven is now**. Hey, He may want to take you right to heaven, too. Is that so bad?

The bigger issue is this: In *this* season it is obvious that our priorities must and will shift permanently. If we are approaching the return of our Savior, then things will have to happen quickly, suddenly, and according to scripture, most likely, catastrophically. You may never be able to heat your home again. But worse, you may lose your home completely. You may end up being escorted to a "special camp." There are plenty of dire scenarios. I believe the Body of Christ will be victorious as long as we are on this earth; if, that is, we aren't loitering around here assuming we'll be removed in a Rapture before anything "bad" happens. It's already that bad, folks.

But here's the Good News: you will make it if you're prepared *spiritually.* You'll be prepared to live and prepared to die, and give glory to God for either option. We're surrounded by a great many witnesses who can say the same thing to us this very day. The ones we can talk to are still alive and need our prayers.

We have been forewarned, forearmed, and foretold things to come. It may not look too appealing. A soldier once told me a Marine quip that supercharged my spirit: "Well, boys, the enemy has us surrounded on all sides! **Looks like we got them right where we want 'em!**" I love to see bravery. I love to hear the sounds of a David with his sling and five smooth stones as he faces down his Goliath. And wins.

God is raising up His warriors who won't back down. He just has to yank us out of our comfort zone and throw us into a good *Gung-Ho!* Boot Camp. The shaking will do us good: that is not judgment, that is mercy. I even suspect these Holy Spirit alerts are going on in your spirit right now, aren't they, Warrior. We're not ignorant of the times we live in. Shift your priorities today. You could call it *breaking your soul ties.* John's Revelation calls it "coming out from among them and being separate." (Rev. 18:4) Funny, isn't it? At the same time we are taking a stand for righteousness to help save a nation, it may be preparing to kill us for that testimony. Think, *tectonic plates.* . . .

A 24/7 VOICE

This practical powerful prophetic world of the Spirit of God helps set our priority system in the Rock of Ages. Like the vision of the tectonic plates, you and I need to be preparing our lives and hearts for a battle and hardship we have never seen before. It's comforting that over the years, no doubt we have been through enough to have begun the process: can we see our trials as that blessing? Go through the scriptures right now and find the verses that are preparation for these days to come. Allow yourself plenty of pages because the Bible is well prepared. Won't it be a comfort to know God's 24/7 Voice *then, in the midst of tectonic trouble?*

MANIFEST

"God's people are warriors. Their priorities are in order. They obey so God's will can happen now in the season it's needed. Do Your work in my heart, LORD, regarding every detail. Prepare me for You. I'm not afraid, and I don't intend to get that way for I rely on Your help."

DAY 23
FORERUNNER

What could be better to keep God's prophetic shift from becoming reality than doing away with the Voice of the wake up *callers* of life? Prophetic shift refers to God's shifting of time, events and people to put things in place for the establishing of His Kingdom. Though it takes a long time, His Kingdom is growing while still allowing man's free will. But at a certain point, He will step in to wrap it up. Knowing this should alert us to the enemy's attempt to thwart His plan. There are people who were born to perceive from this perspective. It's in their spiritual DNA. They are the watchmen and forerunners in God's Kingdom. As we watch people walk away from the Truth, or grow up into lovers of rebellion and haters of God, we see the enemy is behind it. Who are all these people who are right now resisting God? Many are brave leaders, many are highly creative, thoughtful, and energetic. Could it be that they also have been called to watch out from God's perspective to warn about the very things by which they have been taken captive? Could their gift of foresight have been recognized and intercepted by *the enemy of their soul* in order to minimize the damage God wants to inflict on the kingdom of darkness?

God's forerunners have been under attack since they were born

If you watch the evening news, you can identify them as the fighters and brawlers, adventurers and agitators. They make noise, they get carried away; they invent outrageous things and make lots of money; they lose it all and begin again without batting an eye. They are risk takers, trend setters, rule breakers. They can be found everywhere from the Hells Angels to, dare I say, Boko Haram.

The problem is huge. It's not just that they are who they are, or behave like they do, but that they **aren't where they should be to fulfill** *their God calling* **in Christ Jesus!** In this condition, they're missing their very special mandate and very great ministry as a **forerunner,** a warrior-class frontline ministry specializing in preparing the way for the Kingdom of God! Through their God-ordered strategic understanding, on-target observation, and prayer and vision, **forerunners** prepare the ground forces **for the world's next direction in the plan of God.**

God has *many* forerunners that have yet to step up to the plate. Holy Spirit wants to encourage us this day, so bear with me. From children with ADHD who seem to fight every step of the way, to prisoners, to adults who've ended up alcoholics and druggies, to Type A personalities, to users and abusers who either think they've been abandoned in life and have to "take care of themselves," or the extremely creative or brilliant who feel they are on the outside of everything normal, or the ones who have decided to do the abusing: instead of seeing where things have gone wrong, perhaps we can see them fulfilling a calling that their nature, renewed in Christ, has them perfectly suited for. God's forerunners are called to be the cream of the crop. They are also, at every opportunity, stolen by God's enemy and theirs: **you and I have to get bold about proclaiming** *their* **destiny in Christ**. They are out in left field that is white with harvest, even as Saul who became known as Paul was.

Laying aside what the world calls *nature* and/or *nurture,* laying aside what the world calls proclivity towards some behavior, laying aside the rest of the world's excuses why God is not enough and His word is not the Truth, we need to see Him as bigger than what keeps us looking at the fallen side. God is the mighty Deliverer. The truth is, even a vicious, impulsively destructive, power-hungry man like Nebuchadnezzar can be humbled, can turn himself over to God. That is what God says. Daniel and Jeremiah especially illuminate what has happened in times past.

The Forerunner Ministry

A forerunner seeks God, his heart is tuned to God's time table and things to come with a view toward alerting the people to change. It is the ministry of the *forerunner* to perceive this God-action, and the groundwork for coming change, and announce it from God's perspective. It can best be seen in scripture as the job of the **watchman on the wall, who because they are watching, see**. They are looking for signs of danger, of enemies, of approaching news. They are faithful to call it as they see it. They do not fall asleep on the job; and it is a difficult job.

Everyone *knows* a forerunner, but not everyone recognizes what they are seeing. We no longer live in walled cities where we need to guard against enemies. Forerunners may march to a slightly different sound. They can seem to be out of step with what is going on at the moment because their mind is somewhere else, focused on a next thing. They may seem disconnected at times. They might speak out something that makes you wonder where they've been: in this world, or out of their mind? You may wonder why what they are saying and doing seems so extreme, or so outside the scope of what's happening now. They may not say it with the best manners . . . after all, they may see something coming that you may not even be able to imagine.

Because they are fixed upon a new thing, an approaching danger, a situation to come, forerunners may have an edge of impatience or frustration they have to rein in and keep under God's hand. Understand that being burdened with this kind of news, they are already under attack, before they said a word of warning out their mouth. Imagine being that watchman on the wall, seeing an army amassing in the distance, then sounding the alarm. Maybe you know entirely too well . . .

I read in Jeremiah for a long while about the many times he spoke, wrote, and appealed to King Zedekiah, *and* told the leaders, *and* called to the people. I ruminated on this and journaled,

Jeremiah's words for *years* prophesied: "Unless you turn back to God and away from your own selfish ways to serve God as He says it should happen, the armies of your enemy will be here to demolish you." Jeremiah suffered greatly because they chose not to believe what he said came from God, even though he had a strong track record of being accurate!

I could not get off the subject, as it was everywhere I was reading. So I was further alarmed when I heard Holy Spirit ask me in my heart, "What's wrong with this picture: **When the watchman is called an alarmist."** I understood. We are living in those days. These days. Today. Our kings are Zedekiahs, our leaders are blind, and anyone warning of approaching calamity from the sins that are destroying us is considered an alarmist.

Forerunners are prophetic in a practical way, the watchmen on the wall who hear and see what's coming. They alert the people. This gift from God should be nurtured and encouraged by leadership. A calling as a forerunner is a priceless ministry. The Church needs to step up to raise up this calling in people when they see it, for the benefit of the Church. Though their message makes us uncomfortable when they cry, *Danger!* we need to heed them and go into prayer for God's directions.

If what you read here pricks your heart, if it comes closer to home than you imagined, it may be that God has called *you* a forerunner, and it is just now coming clear. Believe me, it will change everything. You will now sense the anointing where before you were squelched. Where you were disappointed, you now understand you are appointed to this charge. It will set you free to walk closer into the presence of God and know you are destined to become who you are supposed to be. The one condition you'll have the most trouble with is: LOVE. Fulfilling this call in God's love.

For those of you who now suspect you have forerunners as husbands, wives, or children . . . nurture the gifting in them:

- Get into a church that recognizes the prophetic, that encourages and trains people to pursue God for their callings
- Seek God on their behalf, even in their presence
- Tell them they have a gift in how they are, and that is why you are going to train them up to fulfill it in Christ
- Declare at every opportunity that God wants to raise them up to impact the world
- Teach them by your lifestyle how to rule and reign in Christ

Today, if you're ready for a change of perspective that can be life changing, encourage your own heart and read Daniel, chapters 1–4. Read it all to get the most bang for your buck in realizing what kind of man he was; we're talking **miracle** here: read about *Nebuchadnez-zar's Restoration.*

"And at the end of the days I Nebuchadnezzar lifted up mine eyes unto heaven, and mine understanding returned unto me, and I blessed the most High, and I praised and honored him that liveth for-ever, whose dominion *is* an everlasting dominion, and his kingdom is from generation to generation:

And all the inhabitants of the earth *are* reputed as nothing: and he doeth according to his will in the army of heaven, and *among* the inhabitants of the earth: and none can stay his hand, or say unto him, What doest thou?

At the same time my reason returned unto me; and for the glory of my kingdom, mine honor and brightness returned unto me; and my counselors and my lords sought unto me; and I was established in my kingdom, and excellent majesty was added unto me. Now I Nebuchadnezzar praise and extol and honor the King of heaven, all whose works *are* truth, and his ways judgment: and those that walk in pride he is able to abase." (Dan. 4:34–37)

A 24/7 VOICE

What you're looking at here may just be the beginning of a huge, long anticipated, life-altering change you have been praying for in someone's life. Maybe your own. Don't just think about it: write it down! Make the vision plain so you can see it clearly. Press into prayer because God has a clear vision of what you need to know next! (Hab. 2:2) The world is poised for the next shift toward God's wrapping things up: we need to know our forerunners and our fore-runners need to know we need them.

MANIFEST

"God has an assignment for me. I stand in faith that I shall fulfill His plans for, in, and through me. I will be helpful and strong in Your Kingdom!"

DAY 24
VISIONS, DREAMS, AND PROPHETIC INTERCESSIONS

"Wherefore he is able also to save them to the uttermost that come unto God by him, seeing he ever liveth to make intercession for them." (Heb. 7:25)

Today, as we talk about visons, dreams, and other Kingdom workings, let's automatically assign to them a place of prophetic assignment to intercede. Our Spirit-appointed purpose in the earth is accomplished by God as: He calls us **awake**, we become **devoted**, aware, and assigned for duty on behalf of a lost world. This life becomes our **manifesto**, our mission and the marvel of God as He works it out. Dear *LORD*, what a calling!

What you accurately see will then become a help because you have been changed into that help. This is everyday life, and it is prophetic. In Christ, the prophetic becomes *salvation*. Outside of Christ . . . the prophetic becomes a problem. In the world a wrong, inaccurate, perverted prophetic message from something other than the spirit of Jesus is death.

Dreams and visions open heaven's wisdom to your mind

Let's totally enjoy living in this practical, powerful, prophetic, calling! Today might be the chapter you most wanted to start with when you saw the words *dreams* and *visions*. What do *you* see when you see? Let's jump into the river here and find the flow of God that reaches us with life.

Sometimes dreams or visions are full color, full-story, filled with prophetic meaning. They're intense, real, active, time sequenced, and plotted—like watching a movie. Other times, they are snippets, lacking color, with a meaning I have to seek God for a precise explanation. What about you? Write your dreams and what you have seen that seems visionary in your dream journal, date them, pray about them, and listen. Confer with someone in the church gifted in interpretations.

Sometimes it's hard to tell the difference between visions and dreams, especially when it happens right as someone is waking up. Over the years, I've learned that I have mini-visions. For a while I missed many of them as they went by because I didn't know what I was seeing or what to pay attention to. Was it the tail-end of a dream I was already forgetting? What was I looking at? What would a vision look like? Is it a full-color spectacle, a panorama, or in black and white? And do they happen in the night time or during the day? Does a vision last for hours while I'm transfixed? Could I be absorbed into a vision for a time or does that mean it was a dream? Does a vision simply appear in a moment like a snapshot—now you see it, and then it's gone? Or can a vision last only a moment but it could seem like hours?

Of course, the answer to all these questions is, *yes,* at one time or another. Dreams and visions happen in many and various ways and formats, times of day or night, lasting for different amounts of time. My practical prophetic instructions from the Lord have been, "You need to become familiar with God's way of speaking to *you.*" There are hundreds of instruction manuals and medical journals about dreams, alone: Rapid Eye Movements, deep sleep dreams, and so on. This book is not about those details. **Today is the call to pursue dreams and visions as prophetic tools, and discover how and why they mesh with the rest of the Spirit-led life in this time** (Appendix D includes a book title on dreams by Laura Harris Smith). *This Practical Powerful Prophetic* is your manifesto for birthing the things of the Spirit in these last days that will be instrumental in establishing the Kingdom of God in people and situations. Our brains are great but our God and His ways are greater.

The shift we address today is Holy Spirit turning our thoughts and attention to the things of the Spirit that have seemed only symbolic, when in fact they were the substance of the real! For most of us, there are crevasses in our minds and hearts where we still hold out on God, and limit ourselves as a result. "The man without the Spirit does not accept the things that come from the Spirit of God, for they are foolishness to him, and he cannot understand them, because they are spiritually discerned. The spiritual man *makes judgments* [or assessments] *about all things,* but he himself is not subject to any man's judgment: 'For who has known the mind of the Lord that he may instruct him?' But we have the mind of Christ." (1 Cor. 2:14–16 NIV) Today's message to His Kingdom is that **we have that mind of Christ!** We should never again limit Him with unbelief.

Abraham walked out the door of his tent in the night. He looked up and saw the stars, billions of them in a black night sky. Suddenly something changed that caused Abraham to take pause! What he was seeing in the natural, he started *seeing prophetically,* seeing into. He was immersed in the atmosphere of heaven as it came close to speak **meaning** into an already meaningful natural sight. In the following moments, Abraham became a changed man. The understanding came to him: God brought it on home to him, it was personal, intimate, overwhelming, grace-full, more than he could think or imagine, an unimaginable promise. "Your seed shall be as the stars of heaven."

The natural *facts* did not confirm Abraham's revelation: he had no child for one hundred years. How would *you* like to wait that long? The natural "time" for that was far past for both him and Sarah. **But he was following God.** God gave him eyes to see and ears to hear from within his spirit-man. He believed, because he had listened and responded to smaller (!) intuitions: "leave your country and go to a land I will show you." Was that a dream? No. Was it a vision? Perhaps. What we do know is that he was just standing there looking up at the sky **when revelation,** or new **"in-sight" came** to him. It might have taken only a moment, yet it forever impacted Abraham and history.

Open Ears . . . Open Eyes . . . Open Heaven

Here's validation for your seeing and dreaming: we are Abraham's family, with the same blessings, including the blessing of having eyes to see and ears to hear. (Gal. 3:16, 29) God speaks to *us.* His 24/7 Voice is ours to live immersed in! And *better* than Abraham, because we live on the other side of the cross, Christ lives *in* us. God speaks *through* us to provide the *ability* to receive revelation that will help us intercede for His will to be manifested. Now many people can be blessed with revelation. The whole New Testament is about that multiplication factor. Go and make disciples of all men. Feed the 5,000.

Years ago I had a short black and white waking dream or vision. I hardly knew what to make of it, but I knew it was important. Here's what happened. Notice the factors I just mentioned: *receiving* revelation *provides* the *power* for God's *intercession* in the way it is needed.

I had an acquaintance through mutual friends, but also had reservations about this person. I explained my position as only a friend, and then began distancing myself, *but he advanced*. I was never afraid, but I was unsettled. To sever a friendship is serious business. But to sever one that ought to be immediately undone is absolutely necessary. I had a waking vision.

> I saw a fleeting image run across my conscious mind. It was in tones of gray and sort of sketchy. I might have dismissed it altogether but it was an arresting picture of a torso with a heart exposed. At the other end of what could be described as a short bowling alley lane, someone had flung a seed pod at the torso. Dirt and dust were thrown into the atmosphere as it propelled forward, bouncing and pivoting. When it hit, it entered the heart and exploded with a puff of smoke, as if it had been a bomb.

I knew immediately what this was in reference to. This vision *confirmed* that the Spirit of God was warning me to make as much distance as possible between this person and me, and do it today. I couldn't move fast enough after that. Soon after, what God had revealed to me, now in several ways of confirmation, was confirmed from outside sources. But it was by the Spirit first.

This was a sudden shift into a new frame of mind: my new normal was settling in. This was a new area of Holy Spirit's reality. Almost everything: journaling, the prophetic, the supernatural, dreams and visions now provoked in me a more **proactive response**. I began to take them much more seriously, paying attention to what used to seem like vague details or random illustrations. I learned the language of dream symbols *that God was communicating personally*.

God valued *you* enough to have sent His Son to die for you: don't you think you are valuable enough for Him to speak personally to you? His ongoing prophetic revelation is proof again and again that God reaches into, speaks into, and turns things around. So begin simply:

3 Prerequisites for Interpretation

1. If any part of a vision or dream is inappropriate or disregards the Truth in a message and its interpretation, dismiss it
2. If the message is anti-Christian in any way, or points to self-incrimination or condemnation of others, it is not what He wants to say
3. Symbols may come from many sources; but interpretations form from the Spirit of the Word: the Truth of the Word needs to be *alive in you*

In this season, heaven's language is meant to come alive in you. When He's there in the center of your soul, you learn to walk prophetically, simply by faith. It's not about you but about Him. It's as natural as walking outside on a starry night and standing there for a while, looking up. "My sheep hear My voice, and I know them, and they follow Me." (John 10:27a) One alive word from God can change everything.

A 24/7 VOICE

If you are in a church with the fivefold ministry in operation, there should be a prophet who can help you prayerfully discern your visions, prophetic words and dreams. Sometimes a church may have a prophetic ministry team, in which case, bringing your vision, prophetic word or dream to them can be an invaluable help. Bring your journal and dream journal. Listen to everything prayerfully and then discuss what you have been thinking about it. "In the multitude of counselors there is wisdom." (Prov. 15:22) **I would not counsel anyone to go to someone who is only spiritual but not a born again and baptized in the Holy Ghost Christian.**

MANIFEST

"I'm Your sheep, Lord, so I know You have good pasture for me regardless how we get there. Show me how to get closer to You. I declare that I can hear heaven's language, I can see the things that are hidden as I know You more intimately. I draw closer still. My desire is for accuracy in seeing and hearing."

DAY 25
STRATEGIES OF HEAVEN

"And a vision appeared to Paul in the night; There stood a man of Macedonia, and prayed him, saying, Come over into Macedonia, and help us. And after he had seen the vision, immediately we endeavored to go into Macedonia, assuredly gathering that the Lord had called us for to preach the gospel unto them." (Acts 16:9,10)

Right there in a night vision, God sent strategy to Paul that had evaded him. As we continue looking to heaven, we're in the right perspective to seek God for His strategies about everything going on around us. In our own back yard as well as nation, we're constantly encountering enemy devices and subterfuge that we should be one step in front of. My own concerns go to our country. The Lord pointed out something that went deeper, "Recognize that a nation's free fall into obscurity and eventual disappearance is not just normal or inevitable: it is deliberate. Deliberate choices are made on every level for long stretches of time, in many arenas. Otherwise a nation need not go down." When He gives us understanding, strategies can then come forth to attack on the level that will bring the needed change. Usually it is a moral change that brings a nation down.

Our culture continues to eradicate the guideposts of Christianity, and discernment is wearing thin. People sometimes don't even want to know what is really true. They may not care at all that what they think is not accurate. They may no longer be able to tell when someone is lying, not even themselves.

You and I are in a special place in this climate: we have access to the strategies of heaven. Respond to the horrific, unbelievable, ghastly, deceptive events you see on TV by going into prayer with a group of intercessors to seek God for His strategies in return. You can *expect* this supernatural help! Imagine scenarios requiring God's strategy in situations that could actually be real:

- You're accustomed to driving down a certain road at night after class, but you hear a thought that says, "**don't go that way**; go this other way." Wouldn't you like to be so familiar with His Spirit that you'll know it's *His voice*?
- You're getting ready to speak to a group about a subject, and there is a potential problem you'll be facing. Wouldn't you like to hear about it, and about your response from God's voice to your heart, **before you stand** up?
- Your spouse has a choice to make about the job. As a couple you have two days to make your decision and give it to the boss. Each choice will have its difficulties, expenses, dangers, and benefits. Knowing that choices take you on roads that change your future, you'd really like to know **which one God wants** you to take.

"The prophetic" isn't some new craze we can make a reality show from. The supernatural and the prophetic are God's home base of operations: it's *how* He operates because of who He is. Discernment and strategy comes prophetically as a result of seeking God and knowing His Word. It all works together. Right doctrine makes a difference between truth and heresy. Leaving off sound instruction is a disaster. Omitting the prophetic leaves dry bones in the wilderness unspoken to. If discernment means recognizing and telling the difference in something, then failing to discern God's prophetic voice means we have missed the most important part of His speaking. Divine Strategies are reinforcements from Holy Spirit, designed to help us wage successful spiritual warfare.

I've been burdened for our country for decades. In the course of asking God the "who/what/when/where" questions I've read hundreds of accounts and explanations of the state of the world. That, mixed with what the Word is increasingly revealing, finally opened my heart to **listen for the prophetic response to it all**. The Lord sent this dream. He gave me wisdom, and I got discernment from it that I could weigh in on situations as they arose. It holds truer today than it did fifteen years ago.

> I was going to see *this house that was for sale*. I never saw the realtor, but was allowed inside. It was totally *empty* and *clean*. I saw the first large room and an opening that led to the back of the house, which was immense, like a *warehouse*. All of it was *empty* and *very dimly light*. I started to walk further back in, but hesitated. To my *left*, came voices. They were mens' voices, loud and *menacing*, and I understood that they were "*dark* men, hidden as they worked, at this time." Whether that meant evil or dark-skinned, or that they worked under cover of darkness, or all three, I didn't know. But it wasn't good; it was dangerous. I heard them working with "*heavy metal*" substances. There was a loud clanging or clanking of metal on metal: it could have been steel, it could have been iron: it could also have had a more elemental meaning: heavy metal, meaning uranium. I started to walk over to where their voices could be heard and the pounding work was being done: it was *behind* a railing and down, so you *couldn't see them*, like they were in a basement room *under* the house. But I was afraid and headed for the door. No one followed me, nothing impeded my exit.
>
> Once outside, the Spirit lifted me up and I was transported way back to a mountain far across the valley where the house was. Suddenly I saw two things: the house was being overwhelmed *overhead* by the mountain it was situated near. The rocks and land were pushing right over the top of it, from the left to right. The walls on the sides were at a 45 degree angle. Then I saw this: an American flag flying at a crooked angle over the house.

I awoke and sat in silence, and the Lord spoke:

> "Here it is, up for sale. It looks good, swept and garnished. It is beautiful and spacious, and at one time held much of value. But it has been sold to evil. It is a land largely empty of real life now. Go ahead, look around. The intimidating voices you hear are from the darkness at the very foundations of this House. They are indeed working *against* this house, for no good purpose. They *are* using heavy metals, and worse: murder and fear. Come up here and I'll show you more. This house is being covered by a mountain that is

going to crush it if it isn't stopped. It has already broken the strength of the House: its walls and foundation. Yes. It is the United States of America, a nation that has lost its discernment and direction. And you are here at this time for My purposes: so speak out, pray, and don't let anything stop you. The strategies of heaven are for you to seek and find."

The strategy He left with me began a warfare on a personal level to get over the fear. It has since grown to a bolder outreach. The discernment He provided me then is still accurate today. It provides the "seeing behind the *seens*" that keeps me focused in prayer and observation **and in response**. When you know what God wants, what God sees, and His intentions, you pray more effectively, with discernment, and you understand better how you will be called upon to respond.

We're looking to Heaven where The God of the Angel Armies has the perfect strategies to overcome and stop the enemy in the situations He alerts you to. The Lord is not slumbering or sleeping. His heart is for His people and for the hearts of unbelievers to come to Him. He has already made provision for you to receive and fulfill your assignment. Avail yourself of His provision. Tell your **attitude, Wake up! You will not atrophy, you will not lose heart; you still have work to do.**

When we finally understand how dependent we are on our Lord, and how strong we are in the power of His might, our thoughts go toward preparedness on a whole different level. Give Him time and space to speak strategically. Then in one accord, move.

A 24/7 VOICE

"I will instruct thee and teach thee in the way which thou shalt go: I will guide thee with mine eye." (Psalm 32:8) Recall a time that you had to seek God for His strategic direction to stop a bad situation. Write about it. Describe how it all happened and what the outcome was.

MANIFEST

"You have a plan for me that You have already started. I shall fulfill it, too . . . not by my might, but by Your Spirit! I have eyes to see and ears to hear what's happening around me, both in the natural and in the spirit. My heart is Yours, God. You give Your people strategies from heaven."

DAY 26
THE DARK FIELD

"Arise, shine; for thy light is come, and the glory of the Lord is risen upon thee. For, behold, the darkness shall cover the earth, and gross darkness the people: but the LORD shall arise upon thee, and his glory shall be seen upon thee." (Is. 60:1, 2)

God prepares us with strategy: uncanny, supernatural wisdom, discernment, and directions for engaging trouble from the enemy when we have to. We want to be prepared when entering dark fields, whether they are subjects to discuss, where we work, who we live around, or where we are headed.

I had a series of short visions that prepared me for three separate incidents that happened soon afterward. They will accurately describe how daily life is often tied into the supernatural. The first I'm describing was a waking vision, which means, as I was waking up. I had not been thinking about any such things as words, bombs and warfare in my own mind, but, "the LORD giveth wisdom: out of *his* mouth comes knowledge and understanding." (Prov. 2:6)

I was not sleeping. My conscious mind was coming into focus that morning when a quick black & white picture flashed in front of me. It took only a moment and it was only a snapshot, not a video; quick and complete. I immediately wrote down the picture I had just seen; then I would ponder it:

- It's almost dark.
- I stand before a large flat open field stretching out before me, about the length of a football field.
- It is a battlefield, but I don't see dead bodies.

- I see alive people sitting alone, cross-legged, with heads down, frozen in place.
- Planted all around them in shallow ground are minefields. I knew this by the Spirit, because I didn't see bombs.
- The people were there before the field became minefields because they got there without being blown up. Now, though, they realize it's treacherous.
- They can't move. Or they won't. Or they don't know they need to? Or don't know what to do?
- *What are the bombs?* I asked, wondering if they can be detonated.
- The Words came to me: "They are the enemy's words encapsulated in demonic spirit."
- *What words?* I asked, presuming they were words like, *hopeless, angry, "I hate," relative truth, rejected, there is no God,* etc.
- Then came the revelation: "Here are some of the words: Holy. Jesus Christ. Spirit. Born again. The Anointed-One. Come-to-Jesus-meeting. Preach. Save-the-world. Amen."

Do you see that? **Every word of the Bible that is the most clearly understandable and essential to man as Truth**—*was now perverted to become empty of truth, dead or deadly!* I didn't expect this at all; it was exactly opposite what I was thinking. I was stunned.

The enemy's mission is to counterfeit the Truth. He has gotten bold in these days where good is looked at as evil, and evil, as good. This is the demonically inspired relativism we see in our culture. As the entire world falls into the hands of evil, the outlook is bleak and will lead up to the great falling away, and the revelation and deception of the antichrist. It is under way as we speak. We could say that *outside* the borders of the Kingdom of God in His Church on earth, there's not much else but dark fields through which we have to navigate.

The media may not be "The False Prophet," but it is doing a good job as one as it pumps out a world of untruth and ungodly filth. You can hear the "gospel *according to the world*" all around you, well-packaged, and endorsed by the rich, the famous and infamous everywhere (and by the way, it sounds really "good"):

Salvation is from within you. Your focused intention, your good heart, your innate knowledge of spirit, positive thoughts, love and light *in you—that's the god in you.* The universe will send what you imagine to you. We *all* see God and know him *or her—*in our own way—and there is no "wrong way" *except* when we say, *There is only ONE way.* There is no good or evil, just different perspectives. In the end we all dissolve and blow away and it is over, unless we chose to come back to rise to a higher place in reincarnated circles.

These are corruptions, distortions, and counterfeits of Truth. They cause no waves to the world, but in the spirit world they are the bombs sent to keep the people of God and the people of the world in their places. There is nothing good about this. *Neutrality* about Truth *sounds* good in this world. Like fine wine "has a nice *bouquet*," acceptance of all things being equal promises a more tolerant and perfect world.

Pretty soon, it becomes apparent there is One voice still clinging to the assertion that it stands alone as THE Truth. How quickly the voices crooning "light and love" turn violent when they hear the voice of one still saying there is only One Truth: "Maybe we *will* achieve world peace if we can get rid of those insufferable, intolerant Christians. We'll keep everything nice and neutral! Everyone can be happy if we all will fit into this plan and keep our mouths speaking one and the same thing." It reminds me of a long ago Old Testament falling tower incident that took down a *whole language* and scattered the people from that day, on. That perhaps is what is being revived here these days.

So, to turn our eyes from the negative to **the positive announcing of the Kingdom of God**, passionate prophetic words are aimed by Holy Spirit to reach a target market that He wants to survive, revive, and thrive in His Spirit. More and more are listening, hearing, and seeing the Truth: He is *jealous* for us in a laid-down-His-life way. Praise God—His love is aggressive, personal, verbal, direct, insistent, compelling and amazing! He feels that way about *all* people and whosoever hears this heart tone of His can be set free. That's why He will give us Spirit-led ideas on how to reach people around us: on-time knowledge from the Throne Room that tells the Truth. His heart breaks that there is coming a day soon when, "While people are saying, 'Peace and safety,' destruction will come on them suddenly, as labor pains on a pregnant woman, and they will not escape." (1 Thess. 5:3 NIV) It should break our hearts into supernatural saving action.

A 24/7 VOICE

Jesus said, "Occupy till I come." Write about the ways He has shown you to not only take the territory He wants you to occupy, but how to keep it. This need not be a list of aggressive actions (but it might be), but perhaps things the Lord has spoken to you about concerning your nature and temperament. Everyone is different, so a journal entry like this will be a you-and-God entry. His voice will incorporate the things going on around you as a tie-in.

MANIFEST

"God, You are not neutral about the things You care about, and that is pretty much everything! Your Kingdom is light, and in You is no darkness at all. Open my eyes to see where my attitude needs to adjust to You. I need you to strengthen me to do Your will."

DAY 27
HEARING GOD SAVE

"Thy testimonies have I taken as a heritage forever: for
they are the rejoicing of my heart." (Psalm 119:111)

God has given us the treasure of His written Word from the beginning of man's journey through earth time. Do we *hear it saving us all the time*? He also has sent all kinds of supernatural meetings and interactions. Do you *hear them and see them*? We were never meant to "just get hold of His Word and just do it." His ongoing input is the whole point, in a very personal level. The ears He tells us to hear with are our spiritual ears, open to Him! The supernatural is His stamp of authenticity: signs and wonders follow those who believe. (Mark 16:17, 18)

If God gives you a vision, a word, a dream, He wants you to *get* something from it and *take* it somewhere. Ask. Listen. Write it down. Get in the Word. Pray. Search out the dreams and visions in the scriptures. Get comfortable thinking about the prophetic.

When we have so many options on so many levels at all the same time, we've been conditioned to not respond by faith; maybe not respond at all: it's all too much. Get alone with your Lord.

Get rid of unbelief. It comes from all the stuff you hear around you that tidily excludes the Truth. Today, let's exclude unbelief and watch how He saves the day. It comes in the form of quasi-biblical teaching: "well, no scripture is prophetic until it is fulfilled." The entire Word of God is prophetic: before it is seen it is fulfilled, and visibly, after it is fulfilled. From eternity.

How dare I think God's Word can only be prophetic after I have verified it as so? It doesn't revolve around me or men's opinions. But just so we can know God *is* the God of all truth, *if we have ears to hear and eyes to see,* He shows us the proof we need, we get to discover it *as* He reveals. But blessed is the man who believes it first, before he sees it (John 20:29).

So let's go back to the vision I had of *The Dark Field,* because it is here that the seeds of unbelief are sown and then explode like weeds. What was I to do with this vision? What did God mean by it? I had seen and heard the negative, but I needed *to hear God save.*

> "Suddenly I saw pops of light—like explosions—burst forth all around the people near and far, out of the ground around them! Again I asked what was happening, and the Lord said to me,
>
> - "This is what's happening: I want you to go in. *Take back My Words.* Re-*form* them into the words of Life—*Re-form what has been de-formed.*"
> - Then came the verse in Matt 4:16 (NASB): "the people who were sitting in darkness saw a great light, and those who were sitting in the land and shadow of death, upon them a light dawned."
> - My last question was, *HOW* do You want me to take back Your words?!"

Here is how the prophetic opens up from the Spirit of God and His Word:

1. God gives a vision or a dream
2. You submit it to Him, asking for any other information
3. He speaks His revelation-mind
4. The Scriptures confirm everything
5. You ask Him to interpret, direct, guide, work it, etc.

Then what happens? Not by coincidence, soon after this vision He began to open my eyes to situations that were happening **all around me every day in which words had become de-formed**. It was worse than I thought. The first opened up the very next night at a party.

> I was at a friend's home (he's a teacher). He was showing us photos of a school event and came upon a student. He told us that this little fella wasn't allowed by his religion to pledge allegiance

to the flag. (I figured the child may be from a hostile country). He said the boy was a Jehovah's Witness, and began to describe their religion . . . *no holidays, no pledge of allegiance,* etc. He then said, heatedly, 'this is a cult and a blight on the name of Christianity!' He himself is not a born again Christian, and doesn't know the difference because he doesn't want to know there is a difference–he practices his Catholicism along with Buddhism, Transcendental Meditation, and New Age positivism. The One-World religion.

Here in front of me was a picture of **culture mash at its religious best, the stuff of what is coming, and already *is*.** Wake up call. Same evening, we were looking at photos of a couple's recent trip to Europe. When we began to look at photos of churches in Spain, they and another friend, who *is* born again, *both* remarked about one church in particular: "*half of it is used by the Catholic Church; the other side is a mosque.*" **All of them wished aloud that this sweet working together could be worldwide.** I groaned, knowing where prophecy studies had taken me. I said, "it soon will be, but it won't be nearly as sweet as you might think." I hoped a little shock value might break through at least to the other 'believer' in the group. But quickly the next photo caught their eyes and the words were lost.

There is nothing extraordinary about this event or the people in it. We all talk to many people as friends. We try to be careful not to step on anyone's toes. We overlook things people say that are inaccurate scripturally (and thus, truthfully). It's part of being the irresistibly sweet people we are. But if we saw into the spirit we would see that "we don't wrestle against flesh and blood . . ." (Eph. 6). Anti-Christian sentiment comes in many forms; it is hovering over the world and even settling down at dinner tables. Do we continue to let it go unaddressed, unchallenged? Is that the definition of salt and light?

*"Mine" fields: where what I live by is "mine": my
truth, my interpretation, my will, my plan*

This sentiment was once the desire of my heart: "How wonderful the day will be when we all can live in harmony like this." I had no clue who Jesus really was and is. Then someone lived Him out in front of me. I heard and God saved me.

Wherever darkness has obscured the truth, there are undisclosed mine fields causing problems. They could explode at any minute, and **Truth has a way of detonating them.** When religion has come to mean that anything you want to believe in becomes *the* truth, there is a collision of belief systems: demonic doctrines, inter-faiths, traditions, flesh, guesswork, and then The Word of God enters. An otherwise jovial evening steeped in culture mash can go up in flames when the Truth comes forth. Your intrusion may look like too much light on a subject for people sitting in darkness and rather enjoying it. Can you see how people may "unfriend" you, hate you, and wish you were . . . uh . . . *removed*? They will think they are doing God a favor when they kill you? But, I digress.

Salt and light are in short supply and your voice tastes of both

The coming season of the supernatural is accompanied by a different climate we've been used to—violence and suffering on a large scale. We've watched it escalate on TV every night and day, for years, and not understood what we were watching. It has become normal to us because we've been desensitized, and not by accident, in case you want to hope that it's just a human nature issue. That it is, but by now you understand it has plenty of help getting there. Switch off that station forever and tune into hearing God save. He IS salvation, present tense, eternal truth.

We stand on the precipice of devastation like never before: wars, rumors of wars, natural disasters, earthquakes, pestilence, food shortages, offenses, wickedness. When they come to your neighborhood, your loved ones, your health, food supply, and pocketbook, **the concept of God suddenly has your attention.** We're *here* in *this* season to take back His Words, to re-form what's been de-formed while we have a chance.

A 24/7 VOICE

"I *am* the LORD thy God, which brought thee out of the land of Egypt: open thy mouth wide, and I will fill it." (Psalm 81:10) No writing here. Just **say something true** today to someone who needs to hear it. Your prophetic practice is to put it in terms Holy Spirit suggests to you on their behalf. Remember, if you are created in God's image and filled with His Spirit, everything you do becomes prophetic: what you say, attitudes you display, motions: a handshake, a gesture, song. That explains the response action in human interaction.

You are prophetic like your heavenly Father. That should open up a few options for how you can bless someone. Giving is a huge prophetic gesture: your time, your ear, a visit, a card, etc. See everything you do as prophetic and your life will clean up dramatically. Strength will come forth. You mean something far greater than you might think. So does everything you say and do. This is your devotional message: wake up and realize you are God's son, born of the Holy Spirit.

MANIFEST

"LORD, You ARE the Truth. I declare I will express Your side of an equation. For such a time as this, I will rise up to hear and have a strong word about how you save. Amen!"

DAY 28
INVITED GUESTS, UNINVITED WORDS

I n these days of prophetic shifting into a more aggressive walk in the Spirit, we could end up being an invited guest at many functions and have uninvited words that quickly turn the tables over around us. That's not very polite, is it? **Yet the world does it all the time in your own hearing** *to keep Who you serve in place.* If you don't believe that, say something about HIM and see what happens. I mean this in the nicest possible way.

I'm not suggesting we all walk around with hair shirts and proclaiming, "Thus saith the Lord, Boy, are you in trouble!" It's not our job to convict someone of sin, isn't that right?

I really thought it was my calling as salt and light, for many years, but I hear that this job belongs to the Holy Spirit. The confusion comes when I remember that the Holy Spirit **is in us telling us what to say.** What *do* we say to a culture that murders 50 million innocent unborn, dismisses Christianity, pumps sex in every distorted form, worships rebellion, and preaches every form of atheism . . . and then tells you that you cannot say anything to the contrary? After the last century of not saying anything, how's it workin' for us?

Today, Day 28, let's seek God about who and what is welcome in our hearts. How did Jesus sound in *His* culture? How did the people of God sound to the nations around them? How did God look in the chosen people He was leading into their Promised Land? These are loaded questions! Going into the Word to get accurate wisdom, discernment, and God-comment is the only thing that will help us be transformed accurately into His image.

First questions, God: How long has my silence been considered consent? Exactly what ground has the church gained by allowing the enemy to take possession by our silence and attempts to be gentle-manly? In what attitude does one wield a weapon as strong as the sword of the Spirit? In wanting the world to see Your love (which is wonderful) have we made sure we have shut our mouths to the way things are, in process, so as not to offend? I'm just saying . . . .

Let's say our job is to *"invite people into a different way of seeing God."* Isn't *that* a sweeter way to say the same thing as REPENT? It hardly matters if it is sweeter: is it how God wants us to respond? Go to the scriptures: find it yourself on every page, how God had His people respond to the culture they were in. It was not a cut and dry, robotic response: it was really led by His Spirit. A God-response is truth motivated and activated by His love. It's not even our own idea of love. Don't you find yourself volleying these types of thoughts when wondering what to say next? Let these concerns drive you to Jesus in intimate prayer!

If we were to ask John the Baptist if he agreed with the "show them the truth by what you do and not by what you say" view of Holy Spirit, what do you think he would say? John the Baptist showed by his actions that he was a man of God's Word, *speaking the truth because he loved*, without any sweetness or spin. Here we have a working definition of salt and light. He was in prison awaiting death and his words were *still* speaking in Herod's ears: an uninvited guest to a polluted party. John the Baptist is still speaking prophetically to-day. In fact, one night in an uncomfortable dream, I saw him yet once again, his voice speaking without words:

> I was with a group of believers and we were headed to a *vacation* spot on a lake. It was beautiful with sun drenching the leaves of bright green trees. Inside the vacation home, by the tall windows where the light poured in, a number of men had fishing poles they were casting in the air over and over again. They weren't going fishing. Children were engrossed in play. People were everywhere *playing games* and it all seemed relatively innocuous. I suddenly saw something fly by me. As everyone was playing games, I thought it must be a large Frisbee. It flew at an angle, up and against three clerestory windows on the opposite side of the large room that had the windows. In that moment it hit, I saw what it was: the head of John the Baptist! It glanced off the wall and its trajectory spun it out

to where I was standing. It hit me on the shoulder and fell away, with all sorts of matter splashing out in different directions.

Believe me, I woke up rattled! Here is how I heard it interpreted. That there are five noticeable things in this dream is a good sign: five is the number of grace, and God has poured that into our lives in the church for such times as are coming.

1. Regarding the windows: the church saw the world more clearly and had more affinity with it (the large windows covering the entire one wall) than with the upper clerestory windows, suggesting a perspective on heaven
2. We were comfortable and happy together, with not much thought about anything other than *playing: playing games, playing at working, playing church*
3. For John's head to be part of this picture (coming into my sites from lower left to upper right) cut dramatically into my sense of reality! It went from the earth side to the heaven side in one razor sharp moment
4. Someone had flung it away from them, suggesting they thought it quite out of place. For it to careen into me was the most startling part of the scene. It demanded a response from me: is his brand of ministry out of place to me?
5. The other startling thing was that no one seemed concerned or interested; they were still there for a good time

I was not hurt, I did not cry, I wasn't afraid. But something changed. This prophetic picture cut through the daylight and into the Spirit with a mandate from heaven. The message I carry had better be more closely associated with a John the Baptist than with a world full of happy-go-lucky Christian views that make us more popular than prophetic with the world.

Am I an invited guest in this book you are holding? I hope this message is not **uninvited**. This is the manifesto part of God's 24/7 Voice, where words are to become "with power," and actions are to accomplish exploits. We are living in perilous times and absolutely have to see clearly that we are here for such a time as this, to speak into the world this practical, powerful prophetic: words of life!

A world of unapologetic life is coming to us

But now, hang with me here, because here is where this chapter originally started. Let's reflect on today's first thoughts: the uninvited words of the world being un- or intentionally intrusive, and without apology to us.

A friend came over to visit. In my kitchen, as he was explaining something that had him exasperated, he used one of those "landmines"—**Jesus Christ,** as a curse word. Before I even processed it, he answered, "Oh, I'm sorry, I didn't mean to offend you." I thought, *no harm done* . . . to me. But harm *was* done: to him.

I was aware in that moment how the Name of Jesus was deformed in His mind. To him it *was* nothing. No meaning, really, just cursing around a bit to sound off his exasperation. He kept walking toward the back door to the porch and left the room. It all happened in less than 40 seconds. Either I had just shown him the grace he deserved or I'd let a good opportunity slide right by.

Here is the Name of the One I love, Someone of such exquisite form, so perfect in all His ways, that God calls Him "the sum of all things"—considered of no consequence—and where was I? I was *unready* with a heart-response. I knew Father wasn't upset with me like I was upset with me, but as is consistent with the Lord, I had a sudden reminder from the Word: "Preach the word of God. *Be prepared, whether the time is* **favorable or not.** Patiently correct, rebuke, and encourage your people with good teaching." (2 Tim. 4:2 NLT)

Uh, *rebuke,* too?

I asked, *LORD, how do I answer that curse when I hear it? How do I re-form the words of the name I love in the ears of someone who has had those words de-formed?* Here's what I heard Him answer:

- "You could start by saying, *That's the Name I love,* and I'll tell you why."
- "You could use it in front of him, '*Yes—Jesus Christ! You mentioned the right Name! You do know where the power is!*'"

Then I felt His Spirit rise up stronger, in a re-forming way: "Just go all out and pray right then and there (after all, someone was just bold enough to use My Name as a *curse!* Why not introduce him to the honor of God so at some point he might be open to receive something from Me!). **Now you BLESS**: *"YES!* **LORD Jesus Christ!** *We love Your Name because at Your Name every knee bows! We can be healed, helped, and set free! Hallelujah! I pray you help my friend right now with this problem he's just mentioned—You heard him!—and we'll give You the glory!"* [here you could insert any number of other powerful verses unless they've run away]

- He finished with this. *"You* can finish with grace for your friend, 'Wow, thank you for bringing up the very One who can help us through the stuff of life'"

Interactions borne out of emotion can quickly and even easily turn to prophetic interactions **when we are ready**. I know that more difficult scenarios are on their way and the Spirit is trying to pry open my lips so I will be swift to hear and sometimes swift to speak in order to not miss an opportunity. That will mean my mouth will have to be in order. In the right gear for a word for their ear. "Slow to speak" is usually my response when there is a danger of rejection or ridicule, not because I am so in control of myself. (James 1:19)

Let's finish up with three ways to keep the flow of Holy Spirit open when you're dealing with people who aren't God's biggest fans:

This is Grace in Gear:

- If love isn't motivating *me*, whatever verbal reaction I am presenting needs to be stuffed (stopped)
- Don't look at people who don't like you as enemies: they could be God's instrument for transformation, and they could be on their way to transformation themselves. Don't look on the outside appearance and don't be intimidated
- Be on guard not to take offense and try not to give any in your response: the prophetic answer removes that feeling of walking on a tightrope and can free them to see a life-giving alternative

The weather is changing. If something supernatural doesn't happen, it will soon be illegal to speak The Name Above All Names in public. A darkness is settling down in this season: and men soon will not suffer the truth to be spoken. And we want to stay neutral?

A 24/7 VOICE

Would you prefer to be an invited guest with uninvited words or an uninvited guest with invited words? What does "not-neutral" look like to you? Does it look like truth? Intimidation? Belligerence? Pride? Does it sound offensive? Your answer may explain a lot. What does neutrality mean to God? Are you glad God is not neutral about you? What is it about God that draws you closer to Him? How can that very element become who you are, become your prophetic testimony? When I get worked up about a matter, I do an acrostic so I can capture each thought in a place (a letter) where it works toward one word of message. Try it with the word, NEUTRAL.

MANIFEST

"I receive empowerment and wisdom, discernment and boldness. You have made me brave in Your presence. There is no way I can stay neutral and still obey You, God. I've tried to figure out a way around it but I can't! Work Your nature into every fiber of my being and I will be very brave."

PART 5
HEAVEN TO EARTH

PROPHETIC EXPECTATION

"But when Christ came as high priest of the good things that are now already here, he went through the greater and more perfect tabernacle that is not made with human hands, that is to say, is not a part of this creation."

HEBREWS 9:11

DAY 29
YOUR BRIGHT STAND

The ministry of Holy Spirit prepares us for what we will be going through. He is up to the task of saving and delivering, and you are His child! When our path is strewn with damage, loss and obstacles, He plants information and help on our path to be discovered and picked. Nothing, absolutely nothing, can stop the flow of His love to us because he opened the way.

1997. I was not planning this, but simply following His lead naturally. Prophetic art sometimes just happens, and when it does, it speaks healing. I drew a picture of a girl with a back-pack, walking down an unfamiliar path into unknown territory; alone, but beginning to entertain the idea that she could again become hopeful. Here was His touch to me, which I added to the picture: To the right is a little sign above some flowers: *Fresh Starts: Pick One Today.* The play on words came from the Spirit, as the illustration's message is about fresh starts in life, while it is *also* a terminology for newly planted sprigs of a plant, usually taken from an older parent plant. *I needed to see this.* It was my own prophetic promise during a season when I had lost everything.

Once I had painted it, I began ruminating on what I had seen God express right on the paper: Regardless how long it all took for me, this new path was designed for my healthy start into a new future. My journey was not an end, but a "fresh start." It held promise now of a good destination, and end, in a very personally "implanted" way. I "shall not die, but live, and declare the works of the Lord." (Psalm 118:17)

When you walk through a bad season in life where God has carried you through, you come through with a new message. You'll inevitably hear God suggest, *This message is for someone around you.*

Today we should take a path to a very real place we minister: Facebook and social media as a means of both speaking and finding, *and* hearing God's 24/7 Voice. After all, these places are full of life in the world: opinions, events, truth and half-truths, and much worse, as well as the Gospel and Holy Spirit's actions of fulfillment in the earth. I'm planning today to segue to someone else's journey from a few years ago. It will describe the difference and the urgency of life without Christ. It happened over the course of several years. Mind you: I'm not able to say the incident was finished with any "fresh starts." All I know is:

We are a people of message, we are God's 24/7 Voice

Our message is communicated by actions and by words. Not just by actions. Not only by words. It's a lifestyle ministry, it is full-round. Likewise, whether we have a word of prophecy or not, we are still communicating and living prophetically. It's been proven again and again that *we believe what we say!* All of us. Even unbelievers. (That is what deception is, when what we believe is not true).

Some message is going out from us even if we aren't mindful of it. Is our message or behavior creating faith or compromising the Gospel, both to us and to others? This is no longer a popular stand to take. It was popular in the 20th century until a few years ago. But the world's atmosphere, as politically correct as they swear they are, has grown cold to the Gospel. And that's where God gave me a touch of grace to go.

We're friends on Facebook. We've known each other for twenty years, and we're poles apart in our beliefs. That's fine with me, he's loveable and dear anyway. I thought it was fine with him. Our "friendship" has not been unlike lots of other friendships in the world where we find things in common and overlook the other stuff as necessary to keep the doors open, from both sides. No big deal. However, in the last few years, things were changing when I read his Facebook posts. This concerned me. This is how it all happened:

His posts were critical to Christianity and accepting of everything else imaginable. Lately the things he posted were more and more inflammatory about Jesus, aggressively hate-filled, toward Jesus.

- I began responding to his irritation with Jesus by asking questions
- Amidst posts of fine art, smooth Rumi quotes, New Age mantras, and other pop-psych interesting things, he posted increasingly hostile slanders against Jesus, the kind of stuff another religious group would have terminated him for a dozen times over
- His posts took on such a decisively vicious attitude, so wicked about Jesus, that I actually wept at the cruelty and mocking in his heart
- At one point, he posted three cartoons from an atheist site which showed Jesus in a very compromised light and I felt compelled to write back, "Please don't post these things about Jesus; it's not good for your own heart to do that."
- He posted worse
- A few weeks went by. I found out he was in the hospital
- While there, he posted, "All religions of the world are the same: it doesn't matter which one you choose because they're all *dead*; nothing matters."
- His diagnosis came in: it wasn't what the simple diagnosis thought it was, it was Stage 4 cancer. The doctors suddenly suggested Hospice
- His next post was again, "Why can't people just choose a god and shut up: they're all the same—worthless."
- I was troubled in my spirit. It seemed obvious time was running out. This would demand a response stronger than he had heard from me, and at this time of his weakness I could only hope he would hear. But I could not say *nothing* because the grief I was feeling was Jesus' grief that someone didn't know Him the way He had wanted to be known
- I wrote back, "that all the religions of the world are the same, you're right: they are all doctrines of demons [mind you, that is the embodiment of his religious preferences]. But there is One who is not part of the world's religions. "There is no other name under heaven whereby a person can be saved (from an eternity of hell) but the name of Jesus Christ." I

finished by writing, Under the circumstances, I hope you'll take this seriously and re-think what you're saying
- I never heard a response because two days later he was dead

Was there a response? I pray it was a different one than he's given over the years. But I had something **strong in my heart—it was lively hope. It was** *God's* **love for him.** I knew the Lord had led this simple interaction. Had the fear of being ridiculed or rejected paralyzed me, I would have missed a prophetic opportunity: of potential deliverance and salvation. That is serious business. That is the power of the supernatural communication we have with God in the Spirit: *He moves us.* That is the power that brings change as we listen and obey: change in us and in others. I *know* that God's love for my friend eclipses mine. And then there's a world. My family. Children. Co-workers. People in trouble. The nations. It's the Good News many do not want to hear. But many more do.

Holy Spirit has words for every person, a 24/7 Voice calling to each one

Where can we start? A powerful reminder is that as He is for us, so He's on their side, to save. God also inhabits virtual reality and is known to visit Facebook, too. Our first words should be to our Father:

- What do YOU see, Lord?
- Why am I here at this post taking it seriously enough to comment on?
- What shall we do today, Lord?
- What do I need to see, learn, or say?
- How will You get glory for yourself in this?

Facebook and any social media are sometimes enemy territory, where people sit in darkness and spend hours online amusing themselves with . . . you name it. Facebook is *also* a field ready for harvest. You may hafta go in there and love them where they are. They might not like you anymore. They might "unfriend" you! But, sons of God, you're *there* for such a time as this.

Your bright stand in a darkening world will be a crown later on. Let it shine. Use your wits and wisdom. Don't simply throw a scripture at them they won't be able to swallow or understand because the enemy has them blinded. Reason with them. (Is. 1:18) God makes sense. Love them by not being crude back. Go back and visit them to say, Hi. I love to "Like" their posts of talking cat videos and little hopping goats in baby clothes. You know you like them, too. These are people you care about and know deserve love.

In places where we could incur recrimination now or in the future, can someone go back through your internet posts and find proof of your faith? You tell me if we need to slink out of the limelight just yet. Ask Paul. Or John the Baptist. Or any of the prophets. How about Jesus?

A 24/7 VOICE

If you have a Facebook page, go there with the intention to speak the truth in a normal, intelligently responsive way, without aggression, in the love of God. Is there an obnoxious post going around about something you know the Spirit is grieved enough to want to address through you? Does someone need a comforting word from a friend? Anyone asking for prayer? Be yourself. Be kind. Live out loud as an alive epistle known and read by Facebook people. Use the Name above all Names.

MANIFEST

"You are LORD in heaven and earth and everywhere else. You are LORD above all things and every name. You are LORD in every virtual world. Oh my God, how do You stand the grief of even one of Your children choosing death over life? I stand right now asking You to strengthen me to do Thy will! Give me prophetic words to open eyes and ears!"

NO NEUTRAL GROUND

Thirty days is a month . . . long enough to establish a new habit. The season of your supernatural is about to spring open. **As neutrality is exposed for what it is,** your right time and right place for God's plan to suddenly come clear can break forth in your life. I was just waking up one morning and I had a vision in mostly black and white except for one area:

- I saw a smooth wide walkway and on one side was "good" and on the other side, "evil." **They looked the same,** and that was distressing to me. How could I know which was which?
- It was hard to see where the middle ground ended on either side. The edges blurred right into whichever side it was close—*until*—
- The ground broke apart and split down the middle as far as I could see it!
- *Now* you could see the difference in both sides *clearly* but **you could no longer walk in the middle** (think, "on the fence")
- Down the middle was no longer an option to walk **unless you wanted to walk through the fire**
- You'd have to walk **either on one side or the other** because the space between was engulfed in fire
- **The fire was the separator**

To a *neutral* observer, both sides still looked the same, but **they were poles apart now, because of the fire.** There was no way to mistake one side for the other, as it had been in the past. It was a "Choose-you-this-day" vision, and I was to see four things:

1. If you aren't aware of danger, it's easy to walk *casually* where the walking could cause *casualty*
2. God is cutting right down the middle to show us that nothing is neutral in His eyes
3. The coming fire & ensuing upheaval will be the catalyst that propels people to choose this day whom they will serve
4. When the blinding light of the fire came, if you were on one side, you couldn't even see the other side! You need to be on the side Holy Spirit would want you *before it happened*

There's no stranger danger than for good and evil to look just the same. There's no neutral ground. It doesn't exist. It only looks like it does. It's an illusion. If there's a message in this madness, it is to, "Get yourself ready for the right place and time by turning your thinking to Him, now." Here's why: Most right times and places are discovered inside our own spirits, first, in an attitude of expectancy, obedience and faith. This is prophetic activation as it begins to come forth.

Prophetic activation begins, not with God's voice but with our saying, *I want to hear.* Why is that? It's because He never stopped speaking! It's when you hear in your heart that there needs to be a serious interaction and change of location, then you get in the right place to hear! You sense the need to watch, pray, and look for answers. Thankfully, the spiritual season we're living in these days encourages this because the fire is already burning in the chasm! Our *activation* is in the faith-filled action. Open your eyes and see it where you live, where you hang out, in what you give your attention to.

The world chooses super-neutral: we choose **supernatural**

The world of God's supernatural is anything but neutral. The Lord sent me, and sends us, a supernatural seeing—an understanding, a dream, a vision, a word—for important purposes. Here are three:

1. to **open our understanding** to *a key we need*
2. to **show us HIS heart**—*His battle is one of love, not hate*
3. to **provoke us to care** by giving us *a personal vested interest*

Activation **changes priorities**. Happening now all around us in this world is an unfolding of prophetic events that indicates this is the season of the fulfillment of all that remains from God's Word to be fulfilled for Jesus to return. This truth produces an environment that is anything but neutral. To ignore the Truth today is to guarantee the fire of the future. It will be God's "last ditch" attempt to get the attention of sleepers who resisted waking up to righteousness. (1 Cor. 15:34)

But wait! Let's not stop here! People we know and love are going to experience this dividing of ways. Will they know which side to choose or will they think it's all the same: *choose any side, just don't go into the fire?* Can you see that your right time is today for finding your right place tomorrow? Doesn't it drive you closer to the Lord? How can we bear to be without the manifest presence of God? Thank God, we need not be! We might have walked through life thus far without a tangible interaction with His presence in supernatural ways in our lives. But we aren't going to finish that way. Do we really need to get burned before we change our mind?

Right here I am going to talk to someone in particular. You already have been burned. By the church, *you* think. But I say, not by the church or by the Spirit of God. You've been burned by the enemy of your soul, the devil. He will use the church or any other means to steal you away from the One who is Truth, and destroy you in process. If you don't see it right now, it isn't because your eyes are the problem. It is because that burn from your enemy entered your heart and arrested your development. Scar tissue impedes the connective tissue of the Holy Spirit's voice of reconciliation. But God's voice is speaking life into you once again; refreshment and hope flowing into your inner man.

He misses your heart. The real body of Christ misses you. And you miss eternal well-being and peace, and the joy and hope of family, and the prophetic promise over you fulfilled. Hear God's voice reaching to you in your inner thoughts. A burned heart can be healed, but not by separation from God *or* separation from His children. Your season of isolation is being called to give way to the season of your supernatural change of location.

The enemy works everywhere he can, but let it not be in your heart another minute. Let God deal with your real enemies; just don't be closer to them than to your Lord when He moves. For it is the Lord who loves you and heals burn victims and takes them out of suspension and into the life of the body, the waters of life in the Spirit. A healed body of Christ is what He is raising up.

The fires of persecution will open wide the door into the greatest awakening to God in the history of the world. Or wait! Maybe I just said it backwards! The greatest awakening to God in the history of the world will open wide the door into the fires of persecution. Either way, the season of God's supernatural will flow during this time, rivers of living waters that can't be passed over in ones' own strength.

One last thought to ponder about there being "no neutral ground." Fires of persecution may also cause those who have lived in darkness to *choose* darkness. The sad possibility is that those who have resisted the working of the Spirit of God in their lives will come to a different conclusion as to what's happening in the world as the separating of the sheep from the goats progresses. They might be too well-accustomed to hearing and believing the Lie.

There will be an end to all this. We don't know exactly when, but we know Christ's return is a lot sooner than when we first believed. The season of your supernatural is upon you *now*. Don't miss the day of your visitation. Help the people around you not to miss their day. The apostle John infers this could be a possibility when he said, "He that says he is in the light, and hates his brother, is in darkness even until now. He that loves his brother abides in the light, and there is no occasion of stumbling in him. But he that hates his brother is in darkness, and walks in darkness, and knows not where he goes, because that darkness has blinded his eyes." (1 John 2:9–11)

There's nothing neutral about that. It's no coincidence that the greatest book on supernatural revelation and end-times events in heaven and earth begins with *serious* practical, powerful, prophetic admonitions to the Church: "Remember, then, what you received and heard. Keep it, and repent. If you will not wake up, I will come like a thief, and you will not know at what hour I will come against you." (Rev. 3:3) We can't say, *I didn't know*, because in our heart there is no neutral ground. And that is prophetic.

A 24/7 VOICE

When I am left wanting for words (which isn't often, as you see) and needy for God to speak to me (which is often), journaling often becomes an *acrostic psalm*. He helps me verbalize what's inside that way. Use a word. Or write your ABCs down the left side of the page. Just begin as if you were speaking to God. In the process listen intently for where He wants to take you in this: revelation? Direction? Information? Healing words? Comfort? Victory? All of the above? When you are finished with it, give it a title. If you don't make it to the last half of the alphabet, that's okay (but there are some great things He can say to you from P to Z). Incorporate the burdens of your heart, things that concern you, what you want from God. Be honest, you need Him.

Aah, Lord God,
Because of Your great mercies in
Christ, . . . [You take it from here.]

MANIFEST

"You will take me through the fire and get me out the other side, safe. I choose supernatural, not super- neutral. I'm hearing Your voice more than ever, and can even sense boldness growing in my heart: preparing me for the contest to come."

DAY 31
RESURRECTION INSIDE

"It is the Spirit that quickeneth (makes alive); the flesh profits nothing: the words that I speak unto you, they are spirit and they are life." (John 6:63)

Every day is an opportunity for a fresh start, a new starting point, a different track. I'm not a runner and cannot imagine what it takes to even *think* about entering a Boston Marathon. But I've been in a spiritual, eternally happening race for forty plus years. To describe it, it's been tedious and long. Okay, it's been downright unbearable at times. I've fallen and I couldn't get up. I've taken the wrong turn many times. I've given up, given in, sat down, fallen down, fallen asleep, and run from, instead of run toward. Every wrong, rotten, self-defeating step I could have taken, I found it and took it fully allowing myself to think it was the right one. I've stumbled over, into, and back out again. God has never left me. In fact, He was there with me the entire time. That is the God I am in love with, because He loves me. I'm His child, learning to run the race set before me, persevering because He helps me. This verse makes sense to me now, whereas three decades ago, it didn't: "Herein is love, *not that we loved God, but that He loved us,* and sent His Son to be the propitiation for our sins. . . . We love Him because He first loved us." (Heb. 4:10, 19)

But that is just the down side, of course! Again and again God's faithfulness has set me back in the race; and even on higher ground. It has often been done by giving me a prophetic picture, one that is one thing but *speaks of* the things of God you need to hear and see. Three years ago or so I was wrestling in prayer about some long standing situations. I was in the kitchen at the stove. As I share this interchange of my pouring out to the Lord, and then His remarks, catch hold of how personally He speaks. First of all, the words He comes back with are what I didn't expect. But also, there are personal recalls, even of a joke I found funny years prior to this "conversation." As you come into the kitchen, you will notice I was a little dejected.

> I said, "*I'll just throw these hopes and dreams on the back burner. Again. I've yearned for them enough.*" Imagine my surprise in my spirit when I heard this:
> "You'll '*throw*' them? No, you'll not throw anything of the kind on the back burner; and that, in an attitude of unbelief."

I sigh. He goes on.

> "Your hopes, your dreams, your prayers are not slung on some back burner **ever**. They have been presented to Me with the utmost heart, here at My throne. I was with you when you did it. I've been with you when you first prayed those things years ago. Each time, every time, you have poured out your heart: every prayer, every hope, every dream, every disappointment. I AM is there. Not one of them is dried up in *My* eyes."

You'd think I was highly comforted that He even was close and willing to answer. But no, I wallowed in self-pity a bit more:

> "*Do you know how it feels, year after year, to pray about the same things over and over, in different ways, with thanksgiving, with tears, in heartfelt receptivity for a prophetic answer; with authority, in compassion, with bold displays of authority . . . and have nothing to come of them but worsening circumstances? Three years . . . twenty three years . . . forty three years? Whatever it's supposed to take, I must not have it.*"

May I add here that in case you did not know this, self-pity is not your friend? Holy Spirit gently went on,

> "I see that you often give way to unbelief and doubt; you simmer in unbelief while you stew about those 'unanswered prayers,' if indeed they are truly unanswered! I don't ask My children, 'Where's the beef'? But I *am* asking you, **where is your faith? Have you put *that* on the back burner** with every skillet full of heart's de-

sires? Setting them on a *cold* burner; one that's not 'on'? Does that mean your fervent heart is turned *off*? When you pull that old desire or prayer back, is it now an old, cold hope?"

(He doesn't let up till it's done.)

"*I couldn't tell You, Lord*, I said. *I haven't thought about it that way.*"

"Forget about the stove analogy," He said, "after all, you're too old to ride the range."

At this point I laughed aloud. This was the old joke that always amused me.

"Instead, remember I AM a consuming fire. When prayers reach My heart, I consume them and they become My fuel to move on behalf of you and your concerns. They become My outreach, and *My* plan heats up on your behalf. If I will that it takes a long time to be done, it is because there are other ingredients to your concerns that do not involve you. They need My attention, too. It is My mercy at work in every 'furnace of affliction,' if that is what it takes."

God's faithfulness has set me back into place time and again with a prophetic interaction right in my heart and soul. They're there for you also. And what are we accomplishing with all this racing and placing, stumbling and fumbling, turning and tumbling? We're tuning up to God's voice, His calling, His tone with us, His appointment for us personally. It's more than a "ministry" at this point, it's *the mantle*. This is us slowly becoming the likeness of Jesus, who only did what He saw the Father do or what the Father told Him. (John 5:19, 26, 30; 7:18; 8:38) I told you this is a slow fast.

What are we accomplishing? It's a crown that we have worked toward, seeking His voice, learning to hear; a crown we'll have on us to cast before Jesus. I hope seeking Him will be one of those things He will say, "Well done. Good and faithful servant!" You may not think that sounds like much, but I already know how impossible it has been. Only by His Spirit constantly encouraging me could I still be here on track with Him.

Recently, I awoke to recall the last of a dream in which the Lord had placed His hand across my chest and on my shoulder to turn me around to face Him.

"I will give you grace to do a turnaround; I will give you the push to get beyond your own resistance. This is not simply a mind-change; it is a ME-change. It is your God-inspired attitude adjustment. As much as the god of this world would like you to forget My help, I say to you surely, it is the anointing, My pouring out, that breaks the yoke. That is My turn around.

"Did you think you were supposed to get so strong you don't need Me anymore? I can't help but remind you that in some of your worst hours have been our most intimate meetings of the mind. The change you need is not to be perfect, but to mature to be perfectly up-front with Me and at peace in Me, regardless what the outside tempest-scale registers. That is My turn around.

"It's not about your strength to make the enemy yield, either, but about your yielding to My strength on your behalf. That is My turn around. And don't think this means you may not be victorious. I do not faint, I don't grow weary, and I work whole earth turn-arounds every second. Nothing is impossible for Me."

When I turned around, I was no longer facing the difficulty but facing Him. The problem was soon gone because my attitude had turned to one of actual joy and release of the burden. Sure, I could have pulled up a new attitude with some "positive affirmations." But that would be counterproductive: I personally want to know God is the Lord of my life and my good success; not my own attempts, even successful ones. To me that is faith, strength and comfort. That is Kingdom relationship. That is my heritage and reward.

A 24/7 VOICE

Oh yes you did hear me say that. Today, consider this an invitation to intimacy with God, to allow Him to speak to you about a difficulty, *in His words,* to you. Ask Him a pointed question you need a turnaround in. *From His perspective,* receive what you need. Start with a term of endearment *from Him,* such as, "Son," or "Child," or

"Daughter. . ." Enter it in your journal because the words you get will resonate with you forever.

MANIFEST

"You are faithful, and in Your power, so am I. Your power is at work in me to accomplish Your plans. I'm paying attention, I'm listening: I receive prophetic pictures that can help me see what You mean in greater clarity, and that also can be a word that helps someone else. My God wants everyone to know Him, hear Him."

RIVERS AND RADIOS

God's Word is prophetic from Genesis through the Revelation. His Voice coming to your ear to minister His Word and nature, His comfort and strength, is not "of your creation." It has come to us through a tabernacle not made with human hands or your head. According to what God says, He is *anxious* to speak with us and move through us!

He's gone to great lengths already to communicate this, but get those ears revved up: it comes by faith that He reveals. According to Him, He will do a new thing, pour out His Spirit in the end times, sons and daughters will prophesy, young men will dream dreams and old men shall see visions. (Acts 2:17–18)

Our God is *anything* but monotone, anything but a "big drip." His Spirit is typified by *rivers of living water*. Have you walked by any of those lately? That's what you can sense in your own spirit when He is moving and drawing you, in worship and prayer, speaking mysteries, loving you. Hear and feel the waters of His Spirit splash on your spirit and a new sense of refreshment and humbling. See Him holding you close and lifting you up again, pulling you into closer communion with your Abba, Father, your Daddy. This is not your imagination being called upon; it is you calling upon God to get closer, to get into His current.

We can return to childlike faith and live in the
River of Wonder and Amazement

If we begin with a childlike heart that wants to know, we're already learning to be quiet, learning to recognize His voice. **This is our prophetic practice.** We're tuning our ears to hear: and to him who has an ear . . . *let* him hear. Look around you for something that catches your eye or ear.

> That morning I had just reread an old article on this amazing fact about babies that can only be called a miracle: When we are in utero we are "breathing" *water* that filters through our unborn body. *In the moment we are first born*, we can no longer breathe water, our lungs must breathe in air. That's why you'll see the doctor sometimes have to smack a baby's bottom to get him or her to breathe deeply their first breath of air.
>
> Then I thought: we started by breathing water; then we breathe air all our lives? Look at the similarity: in the spirit, the moment we are newly birthed into eternal life, we are now filled with living **waters** *and* the Holy Spirit, the *ruach*, or **breath** of God. Both aspects of God, water and air together, in us, to accomplish what they do.
>
> I put down the magazine and walked outside by the pool just as the pool filter turned on. The still water suddenly churned and moved as the jets spewed air out first, and then the water came forth. The filter had gone on, and it would keep the water pure and fresh.

It was the same lesson I had just read about concerning a baby's lungs. I stood there seeing what I had seen 1000 other times, and this time I saw a new thing that brought a prophetic message to my spirit.

> When the *pneuma* power of the Holy Spirit comes through us, the force of it can be startling, and could in fact, be powerful enough to turn our brains up a notch or two in process, providing us with the capacity for a new language we never even learned, or generating emotion. We might easily prophesy in situations like this. Like the jets of compressed air blowing through the pool filter into the pool, clean filtered water comes next. The breathing out of God's Spirit into our spirit gets things going with the intent that living waters should flow and overflow. It's the action of the *pneuma of the Holy Spirit* that moves the Living Water into and out of us. That's why flowing in the Spirit feels like you're in a river.

Flowing in the Spirit carries us past and through many life events. Sometimes this practical powerful prophetic will look like miracles, other times, not. Our clothes and shoes shall not wear out; we'll be fed by ravens; lions' mouths will be closed; we'll be hidden from the enemy; the fire will not touch us to burn. We will feel compassion rush into our souls for someone that will open the door of faith to lay hands on and heal! Provision will come through an unexpected source; we will be healed immediately after rehearsing His Word on healing; a long-time holdout to receiving salvation will suddenly bend their knee! That outstanding bill will come up paid. We'll see a lesson in the pool filter.

Some of His 2/7 Voice will sound like wisdom: answers, direction, solutions. Go here, speak to this person; you'll find a colt, the foal of an ass and you'll say to the owner, the master has need of him. Perhaps the Spirit will whisper to you, "The guy who sits down next to you on this plane needs to hear about Me. Ask him about his childhood cat; the orange one." Or a dream will reveal what you need to do next week. His voice will sound like unknown tongues, a love message to you, or praise to His Name that encourages your heart. Or it'll look like your dog gazing into your eyes with all the trust and love in the world.

We are not looking to prophetic experiences: we are looking to our Lord

As we approach the end of this forty days, I want to turn to a prophetic chapter in the New Testament that encourages me no end. It's encouraging because of *who* it was written to, for starters. You might be suspecting that I'm going full circle to the beginning of this book. The Corinthians. If God can entrust this word to *them*, it was because it was a prophetic word. He intended for the word to fulfill itself through the One who said it through Paul: to accomplish what He had sent it to do. (Is. 55:11) Come to 1 Corinthians 2:9–16 and know that if God can say this *mind-boggling* stuff to a bunch of Corinthians, this is at least what you can expect!

> "But as it is written, Eye hath not seen, nor ear heard, neither have entered into the heart of man, the things which God hath prepared for them that love him. But God hath revealed *them* unto us by his Spirit: for the Spirit searcheth all things, yea, the deep things of God. For what man knoweth the things of a man, save the spirit

of man which is in him? Even so the things of God knoweth no man, but the Spirit of God. Now we have received, not the spirit of the world, but the spirit which is of God; that we might know the things that are freely given to us of God.

Which things also we speak, not in the words which man's wisdom teacheth, but which the Holy Ghost teacheth; comparing spiritual things with spiritual. But the natural man receiveth not the things of the Spirit of God: for they are foolishness unto him: neither can he know *them*, because they are spiritually discerned. But he that is spiritual judgeth all things, yet he himself is judged of no man. For who hath known the mind of the Lord, that he may instruct him? But we have the mind of Christ."

This passage is like discovering gold, or like hearing you won the Sweepstakes. It's like being in one of those aliens movies where the world has been obliterated. You are all alone. In an empty room, you find an ancient radio, a tall wooden cabinet with the window "face" where you could tune in. You find it works. You turn the knob and over the face the red indicator suddenly stops on a sound! You scroll a bit more: A VOICE! Signs of life! We're tuning in to the sound of the Lord Jesus Christ in our midst.

Rivers and radios have currents

The Spirit searches the hidden and deep things of God and reveals them to us. Your hearing ears, your perceiving eyes, are some of the most important end-time faculties to have. Your cell phone, your big-screen TV, your car keys, and who knows what else we've treated as # 1 will not save you; in fact, they might even betray you. Start building your most holy faith today. A huge and life threatening battle was staged to annihilate the Israelites. Then, on one of the sons of the Levites, the spirit of God came, and he prophesied, " Listen," he said, "Thus says the LORD unto you, Be not afraid nor dismayed by reason of this great multitude; for the battle is not yours, but God's." (2 Chron. 20:15) Obviously the circumstances were overwhelmingly intimidating. God gave directions to set themselves and stand still and see the salvation of the Lord with them. Still, it seemed impossible. It was impossible! But their King was a godly man. He took that word as the truth and he proclaimed their response: "And they rose early in the morning, and went forth into the wilderness of Tekoa: and as they went forth, Jehoshaphat stood and said, Hear me, O Judah, and ye inhabitants of Jerusalem; Believe in the LORD your God, so shall ye be established; believe his prophets, so shall ye prosper." (2 Chron. 20:20) The battle was given to them by God.

When we believe God in spite of the things ranged around us, we will be operating in a current of power straight from the throne! God prophesies to us to believe Him and believe His prophets. Are your ears open for God's business? Do you see signs in the heavens? God knows what is going on in your world. He is Master over "current events." Are you in a church where this sort of interaction with God is even acceptable? What would your church say about the supernatural side of God operating in and through His people? I hope they would say, "more power to you in the Name of Jesus!"

Spend time in prayer, in the Word, and in God's presence. That's what it means to *meditate* in the Word day and night. That's what it means to love God with all our heart and soul and mind and strength. Anything less is a dry and weary place where there is no water . . . *where there should be **rivers** of water*. Ocean waves of water. Floods, springs, wells, and waterfalls of water. "Waters to swim in." That's what it means to be free. That's what living in Christ is supposed to be.

In about ten days you will be faced with the *next* forty days of your life. Imagine tuning in to the *frequency* of intimate hearing of God's voice, 24/7?! Look for it. Expect Him to move. The operative word in your vocabulary during that season might become, *frequency*.

This is our heritage in Christ. Find believers who believe this as you do. Enjoy their wisdom and fellowship. There is a strong current these days in the Spirit pulling us into deeper waters of refreshment with God. It's nothing to be afraid of, unlike a riptide at the beach. It is His Word becoming alive in us to accomplish His plan.

A 24/7 VOICE

Draw a picture of your brain. At the top, label the left side, "Left" and the right side, "Right." (I used the left side of my brain to say that) Enter as many things on each side as that side of the brain accomplishes. Go to the trouble to look it up if you don't know, but here's a hint: the left side is where critical thinking skills come in, reason, ordering, analyzing, and lists. The right side of the brain houses the creative, intuitive, meditative, musical, visual, reflective and imaginative side of who we are. Okay, I gave it to you. Idea: Write a worship poem that rhymes using as many of the right brain elements as you can, and use the metaphor of the radio also.

MANIFEST

"You will manifest the sons of God in the earth! (Rom. 8) LORD, I want Your current to flow through me like rivers and like radios. I want to swim in it and be refreshed. I want to be energized with power."

DAY 33
SOUND OF HEAVEN

These are the days that no one will be able to slide by with a minimally invasive Word of God. We weren't born for mediocrity, but to rule with Him over every threat or foe. Can you hear the sound of heaven calling you to war and victory? Can you hear the sound of heaven shout out His purpose in your plans? Someone said, "God is not an indifferent bystander." Let these words sink into your heart and know that God is for you and not against you, and if God is for you, who can stand against you? (Rom. 8:31) Every day, dare to believe these strong words, and these become **your prophetic promises**.

Early in our forty days I said, "This is the season that's taking the whole world into the fire that eventually will reveal Christ Jesus in His glory." Then I asked, "What's this got to do with the prophetic?" By now you have some idea how the prophetic and trouble or persecution *work together to reconstruct our spiritual DNA.*

The sound of heaven recently caught me by surprise as I watched it unfold before my eyes. Holy Spirit used His Word to minister to someone in a trying situation. Here's what happened. I had been reading Ezekiel 47:1–5, a prophetic passage. It refers to the return of the Lord Jesus when He sets His feet on the earth. There will be an earthquake of immense magnitude and the Mount of Olives will split and water from the Mediterranean Sea will pour in, through the middle of Israel, and head south to the Negev Desert and into the Dead Sea. It is a stupendous image of things to come in the natural world . . . and we will get to see it!

But is this the only time and circumstance we can experience it as prophetic? See what you think after reading what happened. First, hear the Word of the Lord in Ezekiel 47:1–5:

"Afterward he brought me again unto the door of the house; and, behold, waters issued out from under the threshold of the house eastward: for the forefront of the house stood toward the east, and the waters came down from under from the right side of the house, at the south side of the altar. And when the man that had the line in his hand went forth eastward, he measured a thousand cubits, and he brought me through the waters; the waters were *to the ankles.*

Again he measured a thousand, and brought me through the waters; the waters were *to the knees.* Again he measured a thousand, and brought me through; the waters were *to the loins.* Afterward he measured a thousand; and *it was a river that I could not pass over,* for the waters were risen, waters to swim in, a river that could not be passed over."

I was immersed in this word when my sister called me. She had taken a personal day off to de-stress, and was sitting on the dock by the river. She had a lot to relate. Over the course of months, her job security was being shaken and a group in a different building were raking over her life and work; a harrowing experience. The stress was over the top. It was all happening at the same time her clients, traumatic brain injured adults, were being moved into a basement area in the hospital, out of their beautiful group home. What she had worked years to build and develop was being renegotiated and removed from her. If I tell you she had been reduced to tears, of the two of us, I can tell you, it isn't her that cries. So here's how her morning by the river proceeded.

I shared the Ezekiel verses I had been ruminating on, then asked how her morning had been. Then she started telling me about her morning. Her daughter had already called and they talked about birds. She told Renee that she loved birds because Renee had always pointed them out to her. It wasn't a "normal" subject for conversation, according to Renee.

She went on with events of the past hour, "The strangest thing happened when I came outside to the dock. I sat down and saw some little spots on the water gradually heading towards me. The tiny spots grew larger. It was eight swans heading *directly toward me.* They came right up under the dock and stayed a long while, and then swam away parallel to the coast." Then she added, "Then, I looked up and two *egrets* flew right by me! Egrets, *here!*"

I responded, "What's with all the birds?!" And **then I had ears to hear what I just heard myself say. I realized something prophetic was happening** here to help my sister come through. This is how having ears to hear begins as it revs up, and I knew the sound of abundance was not far behind. I listened for Holy Spirit and the words rose up in me. "Renee," I said, "The Lord is telling you that **you will soar over this**! You will get over this body of trouble, and rise above it, with wings . . . maybe swan wings? Or egret wings?" She immediately believed, adding, "*eagle's* wings!"

Then she continued, "And then *this* happened: here I was, sitting beside still waters: the whole river was calm. Hardly a ripple. Nothing had gone by up or down the water in some time. All of a sudden, this *long low wave reared up right in front of me!* It was so **unusual,** so **unexpected,** I stood right up out of my chair and said, *WOW!* Then it crashed down into the **depths** and disappeared into the water!"

Now I was excited. I "saw" it! The wave of what amounted to her troubles, rolling in to intimidate her, to overwhelm her. And then **she stood up**. And it went down. I saw two aspects of the wave, like the top side and the underside. One side was that which was meant to scare her. She stood up and faced it. But the other side or aspect of this wave was as it curled over: *the provision she needs to get through comes from God, rolling in* to her from an **unusual** source at an **unexpected** time, from the **depths** of God's provision. She received it immediately.

This is how the prophetic works together with the Word to deliver us from evil. I'm not finished; it gets better. But I want to ask you, first, which part of our brains were coming to these assessments? That we were hearing from God I don't doubt; but how were we "seeing" this as from God? I want you to understand this part because it will help you be free to imagine God at work on your own behalf. Were these revelations from the left-brain: reasoning, fact-oriented side of our minds? Or did they get picked up by the *right* side of our human brains: intuitive, prophetic, and creative? If you find prophecy daunting; if you think Spirit filled Christians are crazy; if you minimize revelations as being your own "take"; if the things of God wear thin in your mind and you lose patience with them: it may be you need to leave your left brain behind and get into your right mind. Holy Spirit moves through the right side far more unrestricted than the left side. But back to the dock; there was more of the sound of heaven moving in. Fast.

> As she sat there talking to me on the phone, the train track she was sitting not too far from started rumbling. She laughed because in about ten seconds we both knew the CSX transport train would come barreling by. I knew where she was sitting, and it was close. Then it happened. I heard it, and she started laughing and yelling so I could hear her: "WOW!" (Being up close to a moving freight train is rather exciting. Your hair blows off the back of your head, your hat flies away, and all you can see is an enormous engine heading toward you. You can't hear a thing but the engine first, and then the iron wheels rolling as the freight cars whiz by. You can be a seat away from your friend on the dock and be shouting at the top of your voice and not hear each other! If you aren't in any immediate danger you can't help but laugh because the sound is rattling your bones) She laughed, "Oh my gosh, **it's *all* oil tankers!** Ten of them, twenty of them; oh my gosh, there must be thirty oil tankers!"
>
> Suddenly it was gone. Quiet. No other sounds but of birds flying from tree to tree behind her. "Renee." I said. "**Oil.**"
>
> "Yes," she replied. "The oil of the Holy Spirit. Oil that softens hearts. Oil that fills the bottles for a woman who was going to die for lack of provision (1 Kings 17:14). *The oil of the Holy Spirit is over and above what I need to get through this!*"

We had heard the sound of heaven: it was the sound of abundance of provision. We rejoiced! But *that* wasn't all, for there were more "coincidences." [And no, not for a moment do I think they were coincidences.]

> She grew more serious as she recalled the verses I had been reading, and said, "Wait a minute, I am standing here *facing eastward*. And the water is heading from the south. And this is a body of water you'd have to swim to get over." That is when Holy Spirit said

to us both, "**My people are a river that cannot not be passed over.**" He will not pass us over.

There was one more miracle of prophetic wisdom and provision that came her way, hurtling down the track. The next CSX train rolled toward her, **a double decker** of box cars on cushioning material **so they would not jar and break precious contents.** It was the **double portion blessing** over and above all the other signs she had seen.

If there is any abundance in the earth, it pales in contrast to heaven's abundance. And in God's Word, you'll find both are ours in Christ. The sound of heaven takes us way above the earth-plot we are embroiled in and gives us a perspective only eagles and angels can take in. This is the height God wants us to soar in His Spirit regularly. It lifts us above the fray, above the turmoil and noise of the world. We are created in Christ Jesus for this kind of "good save." How?

Open ears. Open eyes. Open Heaven.

Does a good save always happen this way, with egrets flying and swans swimming and oil tankers and double-portion supply whizzing by, even as Ezekiel speaks from history and eternity to tell us where we stand? No. Sometimes it's even better. **God's supply is tailor-made for you or it isn't your supply.** It's time to start believing again, brothers and sisters! Strike the word *coincidence* from your dictionary. Nothing happens that way.

It is time to know our God in His power. It is time to forbid another voice to wedge its way in there with unbelief to rob us of the sound of heaven and the Kingdom of God bursting forth its abundance in us. Today, peel off the cataracts of fear, embarrassment, and cynicism that have blinded you. Think about this: **unbelief is unbecoming.**

"But their minds were blinded. For until this day the same veil remains unlifted in the reading of the Old Testament, because the *veil* is taken away in Christ. But even to this day, when Moses is read, a veil lies on their heart. Nevertheless when one turns to the Lord, the veil is taken away. Now the Lord is the Spirit; and where the Spirit of the Lord *is*, there *is* liberty. But we all, with unveiled face, beholding as in a mirror the glory of the Lord, are being transformed into the same image from glory to glory, just as by the Spirit of the Lord." (2 Cor. 3:14–18 NKJV) There is no more veil. No more separation from God.

A 24/7 VOICE

We have His 24/7 Voice speaking both now and tomorrow, next month and yesterday, in the night, when it's too hard to see naturally, and when it seems too late to; all around the world, in every nation, in every tongue; in nature and science, chemically speaking and in physics and writing; in advertising slogans, worship, art; in old and young, in the Word, and in other words, and in the mouths of two and three witnesses. God speaks loud and clear to ears that hear. Today, look out to the waters and trains and other daily objects, and like Jeremiah was asked to ponder, "What do *you* see?" You'll find the abundance.

MANIFEST

"I will stand up. I will speak out prophetically to my season, to my problems, to my circumstances. I hear the sound of heaven and it says, Abundance! I have ears to hear, and Your voice is joy, fulfillment, and salvation to me."

DAY 34
A NEW THING

What if God did such a New Thing that we could see our enemies as the object of God's intense reach? What if God could do such a New Thing that we would see our difficulties as blessings that will fulfill His word in us? What if God did such a New Thing that everything we see points us to Him, to His Word, to His victory! You know that is where we are headed, right? Go with me here.

"God blessed them and said to them, 'Be fruitful and increase in number; fill the earth and subdue it. Rule over the fish in the sea and the birds in the sky and over every living creature that moves on the ground'." (Gen. 1:28 NIV) It's our heritage in Christ to thrive in an activated, engaged spiritual reality where the prophetic constantly informs our circumstances and hearts. "A new thing" is the miracle of God's intervention to do in us what He has prophesied He would do: now. Today. Not in forty more years.

So let's take a step toward the New Thing at our door. Instead of going it alone in our daily thoughts, or in our small vison that church is simply being where we go on Sunday, let's embrace the larger picture of the Body of Christ. Instead of feeling divided, we need to reckon it so, that we are in a very large and extensive and illustrious family: a *good* family that loves each other.

- It is the place where Jesus is alive: *His body*
- It is eternal and worldwide
- It is not dead, or dying, and never will be; it's alive forever
- It is our body that we are a part of
- From this place in Christ, we are one of many joined-together members
- In this place is the strength of the whole and of Jesus Himself!

We can obtain much comfort, wisdom, perspective, and strength from a Body of Christ that spans all of time, location, nations and experience. We also have much to *contribute*! This bigger picture is much more like God views things; it's also the unusual seedbed we've overlooked for faith to spring further and faster in these times.

If you're ready for a New Thing these days, our new perspective is the catapult, "While we look not at the things which are seen, but at the things which are not seen: for the things which are seen *are* temporal; but the things which are not seen are eternal." (2 Cor. 4:18)

Here are **3 New Things** to embed in your forehead:

- *You are not alone. You never will be.* Quit thinking like that. Take advantage of your heritage and the blessings which are eternal: you are God's child
- This is God's "Season of Storehouse" in His Church: don't think *survival*, think **revival**
- Instead of seeing division, make a revision, *it's time to multiply*

You'll have to choose which voice you are going to listen to and trust in these days. That's what our prophetic practice is helping us step into. The world is not your friend. Self-pity is not your friend. Fear will factor out faith. But we know a friend who sticks closer than a brother, and He is faithful. (Prov. 18:23)

Let's turn our attention to **a season of multiplication** and healing *now approaching* that encompasses you and me, our families and friends, our nation and *the* nations. No, I am not delusional. I'm looking not at what can be seen but at what cannot be seen: the eternal, as it comes to our own front door. This New Thing God is doing is called, *multiplication*. Stay with me, now.

How can this be, you're asking, when the whole world is being diminished? How can things be getting better in the Lord when our paycheck is smaller than it was fifteen years ago? How is God multiplying the church when it looks like we're gonna *denomination-alize* ourselves to death? Is multiplication happening as the church is wiped out in Iran? How many decades is my family gonna stay divided: where's the multiplication in that? O ye of little faith.

The multiplication of the Church is contingent on our seeing as God sees and hearing what He hears and obeying what He shows us. It all abides in the Spirit. Now isn't that a wonderful thing? It's almost like saying, "He will provide."

- *Does that mean, even when my church throws me out because I speak with tongues?* Yes, fear not, and find a larger Body of Christ in the many thousands who do honor the Word of God in this way and don't toss out whole chapters because of small thinking or having believed a lie. You'll learn how to forgive and grow in grace. You grow and multiply
- *Is the lengthy division of my family covered under "fear not"?* Of course it is, and much, much more: search His promises. Every day you stand believing for them is another day God has to work in you as well as in them. If your face is set like flint, if your soul-ties are tied to Him, then you are going to walk in victory and praise while you wait. Their decisions **shall not** touch you, and **your decisions will touch them because Christ is in you in power.** You will have much to encourage *others* with in that place: and that is multiplication. Your children will be added back unto you
- *Will your paltry paycheck carry you through?* Probably not. But you're not trusting in your paltry paycheck. (Are you?) **God carries you through.** And you get beyond and you grow (richer) from the experience!

That all sounds like multiplication to me. Now, go with me to a country where the Gospel is cause for decimation: how does *this* situation look like multiplication?

Increasingly wary of church growth in Vietnam, communist authorities are again enforcing laws against Christian activities after a period of slack, the leader of an indigenous ministry said. In recent months officials have slapped many who attend unregistered churches with fines of $25, about a quarter of the average monthly income of many, said the ministry director.

A January 2013 religion law prohibits "manipulation of freedom of belief and religion" to "undermine national unity," and the people have therefore been subject to an increase in monitoring, harassment and sometimes violent crackdowns on unregistered churches, according to a report released this week by Human Rights Watch (HRW).

Highland people accused of religious 'evil ways' and politically 'autonomous thoughts' have been subjected to intimidation, arbitrary arrests, and mistreatment in custody," the HRW report states.

Leaders of unregistered churches can be imprisoned for as much as 15 years.

http://www.christianaid.org/News/2015/mir20150709.aspx

I'll tell you how it looks like multiplication. Many hundreds who see the strong faithful stand of believers to continue worshiping God in spite of harassment and loss, *turn to Him in spite of repercussions.* **They see a God who is worth living for, and if necessary, to suffer and die for! That is a strong and alive God they see.** The more horrid the circumstances these believers come through in faith the louder and clearer God's 24/7 Voice declares victory to the world around them. That's what God is doing in this new season. We can go through *anything* by faith and be multiplied. In a world of division and "removing" going on around us, God is doing a New Thing.

In the midst of trouble, declare your multiplication mentality: **"I refuse to go down in complaining, fear, and despair again: I REFUSE IT!"** Encourage your own heart, re-fill your heart with thankfulness in faith, and while you're at it, share it with someone else. That's how multiplication looks coming from you. And coming to you from God, multiplication looks like abundance, like provision, like life from the dead. It sounds like a mighty army on its way to do battle and overtake the enemy. It sounds like a ram's horn sounding from the heavens. It sounds like answers to prayers you've had lifted to the Lord for many years. Seize your breakthrough, your victory, today.

A 24/7 VOICE

Today, write a new prophetic decree over your life! God's 24/7 Voice has come home to you and is inviting you to a **New Thing**. Pick up your pen. Where you have been diminished, declare multiplication. Declare the sound of abundance. *Reverse* the decree of the enemy like Esther did. (Esther 8:3–8)

Consider picking up the phone. Talk to a trusted friend in Jesus, contact someone who has severed their friendship with you; write to someone in prison overseas or in the next county; or . . . open eyes, open ears . . . make a declaration for an open heaven and the promise of multiplication on behalf of someone else. That's multiplication.

MANIFEST

"God, I speak in Your Name, words of faith and promise, words of encouragement and overcoming, words that testify of Your faithfulness to do a new thing in me. I am more than a conqueror through Him that loves me!"

DAY 35
KINGDOM CULTURE

"And hast made us unto our God kings and priests:
and we shall reign on the earth." (Rev. 5:10)

D o you have any doubt this is the season for us to grow up strong, soon, and seriously? This is about taking our place in God's holiness and authority. Holy Spirit is moving in our lives to help us overcome! He wants our agreement, our accompaniment in this process, or His authority can't be evidenced in our lives. In other words, we have to "be willing in the day of His power." (Ps. 110:3) **He said His people *will* be!** This is the Kingdom Culture in which His wish becomes our command, His desires become worked out in ours, and we walk into the sonship always meant for us. "And hath made us kings and priests unto God and his Father; to him *be* glory and dominion for ever and ever. Amen." (Rev. 1:6) The Kingdom of God is for His glory, for us, and for ever. It's not something you want to miss, for it is the fulfillment of every desire you ever had when it came to you in a Godly way.

I had three dreams while in the process of writing this book. I want to share them here because they seem pivotal to the Body of Christ and this whole message of practical, powerful prophetic action in God's people before the time of His return.

> A large number of us were all together in a sepia-colored room without furniture, a meeting hall or ante room before the main one. I was betrothed to a husband but we weren't together yet. I could not see him in this room yet, but I could hear him speaking to others about ten feet away and my heart melted. The thing that overwhelmed me was that he was approaching, getting closer. I woke up *worshiping*.

I went back into sleep. This dream was followed immediately with another.

> It was a busy church-related gathering. I saw brothers and sis-
> ters I know from other states and other seasons. All were on as-
> signment. But it seemed they were unnecessary ones, like getting a
> jacket or listening to someone describe their cake icing. It seemed
> my assignment was obscured to me. I was just trying to help, but
> my feeling was, I was useless. So many extraneous circumstances,
> botched jobs, and side tracks all around us frustrated me. I won-
> dered what I was doing and if everyone else felt the same way. No
> one seemed to be "getting it right," from what I or we saw, even
> the ones we would describe as examples of getting it right. It all
> seemed tainted with frustration, flesh, and folly. In this dream we
> were all in a building with upstairs floors.

When I left this dream, it was to go immediately into the third one:

> Now I saw a plant in a large terra cotta pot. It looked like it had
> been a luxuriant thing in its day. But now, it was only three sprigs,
> long and gangly with a few dried leaves left on it. I said, *Oh! It's
> thyme!* [I knew that meant: It's TIME.]

Appropriately, when the "It's Time" dream ended, I woke up. I asked, *But, What time?* How much time? Whose time? Is it for my personal life? A person or earth-related situation? You know, our flesh gets jittery when the message comes close to us personally. I collected myself and humbled my heart to listen. *Or is it the sound of eternity reminding me these days in everyone's lives, including mine, are numbered: 1-2-3 sprigs.* It wasn't and isn't a casual message: "Oh, sure, we know eventually it'll all be over; our number will be up; maybe the world is ending, or someone else's time is ending. We already know that." *That is the opposite* of what I was receiving from Holy Spirit. No surprise there. Here is what my spirit confessed by the Spirit, and His response:

> "Lord Jesus, You are coming soon! Very soon. It's like You are
> already in the room. My heart is moved for Your return and the things

"Daughter, the time for playing church is long past. The frivolous and the profane will be dropped out in a moment. What the sleeping Church has thought of as comfortable and convenient will be shown to be charred embers posing as the fire and fellowship of God. Do not worry or fret, for it's My mercy at work to re-form, replenish, and re-*move* every son and daughter. Get ready to come into the timing and placement of My Kingdom, for that is where I will strategically place you.

"It is about time. Do what you need to do. Do it NOW. Say what you have to say. Say it NOW. People you need to reach? Reach NOW. And Pray, *NOW*. The time is short before the world will plunge into deep darkness; spiritual wickedness will hold sway, making your work more difficult but more effective. Prepare today. But know this, that I AM (is) opening the door I have stood at for centuries, waiting for this moment in time. You *will* see My Kingdom come in power; you will see Me soon."

Hear what God is saying as you study His Word. See every word as prophetic promise to you, and strengthen your heart. Make your proclamation *The King's proclamation*, a holy declaration! Declare with certainty! The declaration of Christ's Love manifesting itself in us is also His Declaration of War against the enemy. No more years of playing around! On behalf of those we love, in intercession for the nations, the world, and His soon coming, get your weapons honed, well-fitting and ready. And remember, "love *is* strong as death." (Song of Sol. 8:6)

The devil wants to get you out of the way because **your faith is in his way!** He **hates** that his time is short; **he hates that God is moving mightily.**

- You're not dangerous to the devil when you *can barely admit* you're a Christian
- He isn't alarmed when you **agree** that God is who He says He is
- But he is *condemned by God* when you **pursue** God and **proclaim** the word and **live** it with all your heart—in

spite of—yea, *because* **of the attacks and pressures you're incurring for the Word's sake**—when God's Word is *your* declaration of war

- The enemy is defeated: his purposes are broken, his works are brought into the light and he is put to flight
- And when he hears the sound of marching, and sees One New Man, the Body of Christ! He knows it's *over*

Declare His Word over yourself and your circumstances. Determine that He will work the fruits of His Spirit into you! Declare that no weapon formed against you shall prosper! Through your God you shall do valiantly! And nothing shall by any means hurt you. Lay hold on eternal life as you go; every step, lay hold on it; it is your ground to stand on!

Dreams, visions, and prophetic words are part of our Holy Spirit equipment. Friends, we may not know the day or hour of His return, but we are to be like the Sons of Issachar who knew the season they lived in. That means we know what is going on, and *what is leading up to what* in the world! And we are prepared with a God-filled answer.

This season of the supernatural is upon us; but the spiritual seasons are changing quickly, just like the natural seasons. We know we are in the battle of a lifetime. Happily for us, our life is in God's hands; our times are in His hands. This practical powerful prophetic unites us in His Spirit for such a time as this. Hear this 24/7 Voice all around you attest to the glory of God. There is no more veil, nothing can separate you from His love. Heaven is coming to earth in His people!

A 24/7 VOICE

If you had to make a "holy proclamation," what would you say? Who would you proclaim it to? Pretend you've just been fined $135,000 for speaking the truth, your truth and God's, in your own store. What do you have to say in return? Today is your day to get acclimated to thinking about adversity like that. Prepare your answer. Prepare your heart by entering boldly into His presence.

MANIFEST

"You give us the words that strengthen our hearts! You declare it in Your Word and you send us prophetic words and dreams! I declare Your goodness and provision over all my life. I declare soundness of mind and health, with no fear! The Name of the Lord is a strong tower; the righteous run in to it and are saved."

PART 6

KINGDOM CONNECTION

PROPHETIC FLOW

"Then you will look and be radiant, your heart will throb and swell with joy; the wealth on the seas will be brought to you, to you the riches of the nations will come."

ISAIAH 60:5 NIV

DAY 36
WALKING IN FULFILLMENT

*"And the Good News about the Kingdom will be preached
throughout the whole world, so that all nations will hear
it; and then the end will come." (Matt. 24:14 NLT)*

I can hardly wait for the day my heart is radiant, and throbs and swells with joy, to see multitudes coming to Christ Jesus! To think this could be happening at the same time the earth is imploding, the antichrist is beheading, and every other catastrophe is coming to bear . . . it's an unimaginable victory that will be the glory and lifter of our heads! This is the season to start expecting the extraordinary: fulfillments on every level.

The fires of the Spirit's care and fervor is burning through the complacency and waking us to the hour. **Your voice is a 24/7 Voice!** The things happening around us are plenty of subject matter to speak into. Evil stands in-your-face and fear is growing as the world grows darker. Expect the extraordinary moving of God on your behalf right where you are.

We want to see, not only our own fulfillment in Christ, but the fulfillment of God's Words in those we care about, as well as the world at large. Expect it! Hear and then speak what you hear Him say. I heard this in my heart recently:

> All the years of hoping. All the cares, prayers and prayer meetings. All the prophetic encouragements. All our cries for power, love, and the sound mind of Christ to reach us and re-form the world. ***They didn't just dry up and blow away!* They are all coming to bear on us in this new season of the Lord's return. It's the Season of Fulfillments.** Light the fire again. When troubling times come, and they do: We are not to be made desperate by des-

perate times! Rather, our desperation is for the courts of our God, for *the outpouring* of our God's Spirit in us like never before! Our ability to hold onto God does not depend on our own strength to hold, but on His strength to hold us. Get used to it: that's what He is doing these days! The world will not be ruled by babies, but by sons and daughters of God. If we suffer, we shall also reign with *him*: if we deny *him*, he also will deny us" (2 Tim. 2:12). Prepare to reign today, sons and daughters.

What in the Word we will be walking in

For so long, some scriptures seemed so out of reach. Not anymore. Why, just around the globe on the other side, in Africa, "These signs will follow them that believe. In my name shall they cast out devils; they shall speak with new tongues; they shall take up serpents; and if they drink any deadly thing, it shall not hurt them; they shall lay hands on the sick, and they shall recover." (Mark 16:17–18 KJV) It's *happening there*, where faith is already an integral part of peoples' world views. They simply turn their allegiance to God Almighty when they are introduced to Him, and they never look back. They don't even imagine God could *not* answer them: if He said it, they believe it, and it happens. Strange, right? Fulfillment.

Isn't God amazing to be able to turn us, change us, transform and conform us to His image? Did you even realize how extensive the prophetic atmosphere of God is? ". . . the testimony of Jesus is the spirit of prophecy" (Rev. 19:10). What He said, He expects us to consider prophetic on our behalf!

- **Jesus' marching orders**—"Cast out devils," "speak with new tongues or languages," "Take up serpents," "Lay hands on the sick and they shall recover." In another place Jesus said "heal the sick, raise the dead: freely you have received, freely give."—**are all nature, impacted supernaturally. What He prophesied we can do, we can!**
- **Sowing and reaping are prophetic concepts**; sowing is done first. *Later* comes reaping, in its season. These are prophetically operative words: *In its season it is done.* Reaping happens at the time the harvest is ripe, not before. There is

no harvest if it comes before it is ready. And if harvest doesn't come after it's the right time, then it rots on the vine. **Many cause and effect events and relationships are prophetic in nature. They speak of what is to come,** *if ... then.*

• **Our** *words* **are prophetic, both when we want them to be and when we don't.** (Prov. 4:20–24) That doesn't seem fair, but it's the nature of words. Thankfully the rest of creation can't use words like we do or the world could really be in trouble. The rest of creation praises God; they show us something of God's nature, *and* **they cry out for the manifestation of the sons of God.**

For God to fulfill His will in you and me we have to be awake and on the same page with Him. That's what the parable of the ten virgins is about, with some having prepared with enough oil in their lamps . . . and some not preparing. The wakeup call apparently was and is a necessity for all. If the disciples in the Garden of Gethsemane fell asleep at precisely the wrong time out of fatigue and sorrow, then how much more does the world of care wear on the Body of Christ today and lull us into an "unbecoming" complacency?

As I journaled one night, I was again sparked by the world *fulfill-ments.*

> I *started* the Season of the Supernatural a long time ago—in the Garden. I want to finish it in you, My people, and take you and many more home with Me. **It's time for your lively hope to spring forth in faith.** Get ready! It's what you've been hoping for!
>
> I'm calling you in this hour to stay immersed in Me, in all I AM. **It is no longer about the world system.** If you are putting faith in a new season of the flourishing of Christian arts, music, building, science, or study; remember, the world's system is past the point of no return. **You're in it to win it to Me.**
>
> Don't plan to do things the world's way, for *I* will prophetically pour ideas, creations, and solutions into you so that I can elevate My Word, My glory, and the people who bear My Name in the darkness as beacons of light. It will be about My Light and no other. **And you are that light** in the city and on the hill.

Dreams I give you will explain My purposes. Visions I give you will express My plans. Words I give you will establish My mission where you speak it. Expect many miracles in these times, *and believe Me*, for I will surely show up in your gatherings, in your prayers, in your hearts, in the people I pour out upon.

Yes, right now, people are angry when you say you know what is right and wrong. But many of these same people will come to you and ask what spirit is this that you walk in, and why you have hope in this season. It is not a time to hold out with a tame answer. It is not the season to hold on to your life. It is not a time to trust the world system, for it is crumbling around you. It is **time for Me to fulfill My plans** for you.

Every day, seek Me for My assignment. Fall back into My grace and flow with My leading. This is a day, not to recoil in fear of running out, but to open your hand and give of My resources, My wisdom, My healing, My love. **My life in you is the gift** that, when given, will be your greatest fulfillment and joy. Yes, call it multiplication! Call it abundance. Call it! Call it, church! Call it fulfillment.

Let these words fill your heart: do not fear God's judgment, but expect the extraordinary. That is who He is to you! Judgment happens when people decide they want nothing to do with God and His ways. When He backs off at their demand, what spirit is left to deal with them? That is how simple it is. **Tell them so.** Then live expecting His extraordinary fulfillments. "And the Lord direct your hearts into the love of God, and into the patient waiting for Christ." (2 Thess. 3:5)

A 24/7 VOICE

Spend time in prayer for someone that comes to mind. Find a scripture that you sense is for them. For example, as a prayer of faith, choose a Psalm and read the whole psalm with their name in it where applicable. Declare that Psalm, declare their blessing and fulfillment with authority on their behalf. "Lord, You are Jacque's shepherd; she *shall not want*. You make Jacque lie down in green pastures: You lead her beside still waters. You restore her soul!" (You should do it for yourself, also.) This kind of rehearsing builds faith for exactly what you are rehearsing. That means it becomes prophetic. Now make a greeting card or buy one and put this prayer in it for this someone. Deliver it in person if possible. Snail mail is next best.

MANIFEST

"You have an assignment for me today. And tomorrow. And so, on, till You have returned to get me or taken me home. I want for no good thing and I will tell people that is Who You are. My eyes are on You, Extraordinary One."

NIGHT VISION

O n this 37th day, Psalm 37, a psalm of David, can help us zero in on the strength and power of **acrostic prophetic poetry.** Webster's says an acrostic is a "series of written lines or verses in which the first, last, or other particular letters form a word, phrase, etc." What value is an acrostic? It becomes a grid that helps corral thoughts into a complete message. It is a "mnemonic device" that helps the writer and reader to remember the important points.

As the church enters a night season, we have to encourage our hearts today. Using every avenue to renew our minds will prove helpful tomorrow. Communing with God about a word, a problem, an idea, brings us in close contact with His Spirit, where what we receive is beneficial to everyone! This produces what I'm calling, *night vision.* It's like being able to see in the dark.

No one can imagine how God's words to us, and our offering it up for others to hear, will impact people. Think about this: David was in the field writing poems for songs that eventually became scripture! God's 24/7 Voice is in your heart, and from your heart Truth goes forth that sets people free. (John 8:32) Imagine something *you* wrote three thousand years ago still ministering so mightily to people?! We might not call it scripture, but as surely as you were inspired by God, it could bless people and direct them into communing with Him in HIS Word.

Psalm 37 is a powerful acrostic psalm for such a time as we are entering. It doesn't look like an acrostic poem to us because the Hebrew language has different letters, words, and word order in sentences. The important thing to understand is that in the structuring of an acrostic grid using letters or words, David's gifting with words, sound, and music *were free to well up* from his heart, roll off his tongue and flow through his pen.

The prophetic word we call Psalm 37 entered the world to minister strength to us all, for these years; not just once, but over and over again. That is how a creative prophetic anointing of God looks. If your heart is to help more people than simply yourself, by encouragement and on-time words from Holy Spirit, in song, ministry or poem, this practical, powerful, prophetic exercise is for you.

David *was* fretting because of evildoers and workers of iniquity. But he knew he'd be in trouble if he stayed on those thoughts. As he considered his plight, he also considered the ways He already knew God's character:

- He knew the Torah and other biblical accounts by heart, having *heard them* all his life
- God's presence had been in circumstances *he'd already experienced*
- He *knew God's voice* and allowed *the Spirit of the Lord* to speak

He wasn't a complainer but a scribe that day. God and David had a meaningful conversation that changed his mind and still speaks to us today. It built David up in a powerful way when victory came, too. "Commit thy way unto the Lord; trust also in Him and He shall bring it to pass." (vs. 5)

It's not a weakness to need God desperately;
it's the foundation of our strength

Today, read Psalm 37 for yourself. You'll see it with new eyes and hear with open ears, and heaven will open to you with new revelation. Holy Spirit will gain ground in your stand.

At the end of 2014, Holy Spirit came in power in our church as people drew closer to Him than ever before. We all seemed to recognize we were entering, as a group, a season of preparation. He gave me an acrostic psalm that prophetically began what this new season has continued to bring forth in my life, the church's life, and subsequently this book. *Night Vision* descends **from Z to A**, a sort of countdown to take-off. I didn't bold every letter of the acrostic ABCs, but a few will let you see how it works. It starts as if we're wrapping up the tent where we've lived and are hearing Him give His last orders as we head into this new season. It's a time of letting go the things we've held to; a time of testing, many falling away, and challenges in the world. It's *all shaking up the world to blow in the wind of prophetic fulfillments*! Are you ready to fall back—into the future—with God catching you as you lean into His grace?

Night Vision

Zero in on what's important now. My Words in
Your heart wrap up your part in this next season. I'm
e**X**pressing My will, announcing My time,
Wielding My sword, capturing your
Victory, declaring each strategic move, directing your night vision.
    You will not be
Unprepared. For those
That refuse and neglect to allow Me to build their house—they will
    be unprepared. But *I*
Started this work in you and I will finish it, complete it. *I, only I,*
    started this "Home
Renovation," this Kingdom restoration, and I intend to see it through.
    I'm
Quite sure that greater is He that is within you than he that has
Polluted the world and left his stamp with a heavy boot: *but are you
    sure*?!
Oh My people, make sure darkness has no part in you,
No root in your heart, strong-holding you; no offense that can
Move you over into his camp. This is the season for My
Love to be activated—a sudden deluge, a flood, like the
Kind you find in *the anointing that breaks the yoke*!
Just as in the dark you must have help to see what you aren't familiar
    with,
I am outfitting you in this season with MY night vision!
Hold fast, be healed, gather heart, see in the night,
Go out and light the darkness with the vision I give you—*I* will
Fight for you, fend off the enemy, and fulfill My plans and purposes,
    Hallelujah!
Expect it now, in this time, for at the door is a

Dark day. BUT, you will rejoice, for it is the season of My power, and
My people shall be willing; see what I mean? *My voice* will be
your night vision.
Call upon Me, for I am near—no fear, you hear?
Bring your heart and lay it upon Mine.
Arise to a new season: in the night—*vision*—where My light shines
through you.

This psalm is a battle brief, a strategic order, and plans laid on the
table. Line after line the season describes itself; we see it in our lives
as it presents itself daily. Three clues lead us to activating our "night
vision."

1. Personal history is **a "substance"** that proves to our heart
   we've experienced God: we can **live alive in God's present-
   tense** *by faith to form daily history*
2. A **sense of urgency calls us**, of **time-sensitive** material being
   sent forth that **we must grab hold of and live** *in the now*
3. We are part and partner with God in this and **He will be in
   us** *to walk it out*: We are to **expect** it, **declare** and **demand** it.

All this came out of the "war room" of communion with the Lord
who wants to show us things to come. "Call to me and **I will answer
you** and tell you great and unsearchable things you do not know."
(Jer. 33:3) In this meeting, it's not just that we are invited to sit with
God at His table; it's not just that we sit in His presence and rest; it's
not just that we who are famished may feast; it's not just that we eat
and are satisfied. It is that we sit down with God and rise a priest, a
king, a warrior, a healer: forgiven, commissioned, identified as sons
of God.

A 24/7 VOICE

This is the day for *your* "night vision" to be activated. List those
ABCs. To the right of each letter, describe the process. Describe what
you know you need; then listen for what God says you need. It will
be personal to you, and it will be strong revelation, blessing, encouragement and no condemnation. It is time for reversing the cursing.

MANIFEST

"God, Your promise is that the battle of a lifetime has already been won! You do not faint or grow weary, and neither will I because my help is in You. The world takes orders from prophetic words written into time thousands of years ago, so our night season is going to be an adventure."

DAY 38
KINGS AND QUEENS

*"And there came a voice out of the cloud, saying, This is my beloved Son: **hear him**." Luke 9:35.*

God didn't say, This is My beloved Son, *trust* Him. He didn't say, *serve* Him. He didn't say, *watch for*, bow to, or run with, Him. Are those things not important? No, they're absolutely essential, and in light of that we're to grasp the immensity of the simple words He did use. **He said, *Hear* Him.**

"It is the glory of God to conceal a thing: but the honor of kings is to search out a matter." (Prov. 25:2) It's an everyday choice to hear God's 24/7 Voice for every person, but only His kings and queens will go to the trouble to search them out when they are obscured in some way. The Pharisees might have begun by searching and listening for Him, but eventually, became rigidly stuck in their interpretations, liberally mixed with the world system they grew to love, *and* their agendas. They were so immersed in presumption that they **missed the living Word right in their midst.** (John 5:39, 40) They had no regard for what didn't fit into their rules and pre-conceived notions. Somewhere in their hearts they should have sought God for such an important possibility as Jesus being the Christ.

The Bible will finally come alive

The "voice of God" means the red letters. It means hearing Jesus. It means the fulfillment of His Word from beginning to end. We are to be listening intently, and that requires personally knowing the voice of His Spirit. It will come to our spiritual ears and eyes as perception, revelation, and understanding on a new level. This is for every member of the Body of Christ, not to come under an old way, but to rise to the place of honor God has for His Word. He is lord over our hearts, His life is written in hearts and not in rule books. "This *is* the covenant that I will make with them after those days, saith the Lord, I will put my laws into their hearts, and in their minds will I write them." (Heb. 10:16) This action on God's part transforms us. After all, if we're no different to the world, what good are we to the plan of God to bring Salvation? Why would they listen to you or obey you?

Kings learn authority by coming under the tutelage of the King of kings. Did you realize obedience is a *prophetic practice*? The calling of a king and priest is to **be** a real, acting king and priest unto God. Jesus is training us to be like Him: can there be any more prophetic, more alive, more powerful instruction? He will bring to pass the words spoken in the beginning. (Gen. 1:26) This eternal message of Kingdom life is a deal-breaker. It means our "old time religion" is just that: old and religious.

This practical powerful prophetic life is **your new normal**. If you choose to live this way it becomes your honor and lifestyle. There is nothing *fast* about this process. Your whole life becomes immersed in the Holy Ghost, brimming with life, swimming in truth, washed in His Word. From God's words . . . to our hearing . . . from God's illustrating . . . to, we, seeing. It's a continuous loop of purified, energized revelation pouring forth from His Word, into and back out of our inner man, via Holy Spirit. It's the result of Holy Spirit living in our spirit. Transformation into kings and queens. A kingdom of kings and priests.

And we live to see

Re-mind your "self," O king and O queen: "*Believe* you have a destiny! You *will* leave your mark on this generation." This is the season of the restoration of all things. As the world system heads closer to extinction, the people of God will see His glory like never before. "But **seek ye first the kingdom of God, and his righteousness**; and **all these things shall be added** unto you." (Mat. 6:33) Whatever you have lost over the years by living as an unclaimed king and queen is being restored in this season. Pick up your mantle, put on your crown, put those robes of righteousness back on and expect God to conform *you*, and what pertains to you, to His image!

Apprehend it, apply it, **B**all it up in your fist and enjoy it . . . but you **C**an't hold it down forever, or stop it, or **D**e-rail it. It's not for **E**ver, you know, or even **F**or a long while, *this time of your life*. Life is your season to grow and give what is you.

Go ahead and have it as you can; **H**old it, hope in it, handle **I**t, move things into it and out again. **J**udge accurately what is time's best usage for a **K**ing, for a Queen, made in God's **L**ikeness! For such a time as this, **M**ove yourself in time to do what you hear from Me, and then move again, **N**ot looking back after the time is **O**ver. Just pack it up and **P**roceed deliberately and surely; like a **Q**ueen or a King moves across the **R**oyal floor. Life is a season.

Here is the **S**ecret for having the time of your life: I tell you, **T**hy times are in My hands. In all seasons and conditions, **U**nder all circumstances, your life and times are in My hands. I **V**iew the time of your life as precious. You may see a **W**rinkle in time that distracts or even dismays you, but I e**X**pect all of eternity to come to **Y**ou, as needed and asked for, to fulfill your time in your season.

You have and hold a fistful, but know that *My Times* are **Z**ooming in on you: My purpose, destiny, provision, and a glorious finish.

He ended it with the statement, "Kings and Queens in My courts will have the time of their lives."

His assigning to ambassador-hood in our hearts *with the message of the Kingdom* is our heritage in Christ, **so quit pushing it away**. When a king or queen *decrees*, they are prophesying an outcome they have already seen in the Spirit and from the Word. We *must* decree it as ambassadors of the Kingdom! Who else will? God? We already know people can't hear Him till they turn to Him with all their hearts. Say it: "Because the Kingdom of God is this way, it *shall be this* way!" Say it to lifestyles, to sin, to the weather, to nations, to the enemies of God, to people looking for good news from a far country. We have all of His Word to decree into the world, into lives and situations. We start with what He says in His Word, but He doesn't stop there: there is the fulfillment of His Word to expect. (Is. 55:11)

God's idea of *ruling and reigning* is so much more honorable than "lording it over" others and others' stuff. In this season of entitlement thinking in the world, in that selfish application *of valuing what you want to* the point of absurdity, we see **the enemy's counterfeit of God's calling**. The "guaranteed benefits" of the Kingdom of God come with a season of new *bearing*: bearing patiently, bearing all things, bearing spiritual children, bearing up under pressure, bearing much fruit. **So we will carry ourselves with His sovereign bearing.**

His calling in this season is to rise to the level of the Son of God's type of life. When Jesus healed, He didn't beseech God for healing to flow. He **commanded sickness to leave**! When He met up with need, if the people received Him with appreciation and honor, nothing stood in their way to healing. If indeed the Spirt of the Lord is upon us, it's time today for us to rise up and declare **He** is LORD and not sickness, lack, disease, poverty, deception or evil. (Is. 61:1–5) Prophesy to conditions: "You stop now! In the Name of the Mighty One, **Jesus**!" It's the season to prepare ourselves for fulfilling our destiny as kings and priests unto God! After all, He's the One who told us we are royalty. Eternity will be dawning sooner than you think because it's later than you think.

"But ye *are* a chosen generation, a royal priesthood, an holy nation, a peculiar people; that ye should shew forth the praises of him who hath called you out of darkness into his marvelous light: Which in time past (you) *were* not a people, but *are* now the people of God: which had not obtained mercy, but now have obtained mercy." (1 Pet. 2:9, 10)

A 24/7 VOICE

Can you receive this good news today? Write your intentions about how you're going to live with this practical, powerful, prophetic calling. For clues, read the red letters. Allow God to look over your shoulder and make a few suggestions. After all, it's His voice, calling, 24/7. "I am destined to leave my mark on this generation." Say it. Say it again. Believe it.

MANIFEST

"Your Word is alive and powerful and sharper than a two edged sword. You are the restorer of all I have lost before becoming the Kingdom ambassador of the rule and reign of Christ You called me to be. I receive this practical, powerful, prophetic gift to rule and reign with You now."

NEW CHAPTER

In 2012 I published my first book, *Your Gung-Ho! Life: The ABCs of Proactive Living*. Even then, I remember feeling like the season to finish that assignment would come and go about 50% quicker than I used to have opportunity in which to procrastinate. It seemed like I needed to do it or forget about, but don't dilly-dally around about it. It may have had something to do with the word, **proactive**, in the title. Or maybe I just needed the extra shove. I wrote that book and was glad I did, because unbeknownst to me, that action opened up more than ministry to others, more than opportunities to me. It opened my own walk with God to a far bigger landscape all around me. That is what responding to Holy Spirit does in you, and that's how He changes the world, one person at a time.

I had the opportunity to see obedience as a prophetic act. Here's what happened. When I wrote, ***Your Gung-Ho! Life: The ABCs of Proactive Living***, it was not about the prophetic, but about living a wildly *proactive, gung-ho life* of sold-out faith toward God. Yet, I knew what I was to write about in the chapter, "*Y is for Your Life, Your Canvas*" was a prophetic word about life in this spiritually charged season. The prophetic word was almost the entire chapter. At the time I wrote it, I wondered whether it was fitting for a book to have a chapter with a prophetic word if the book wasn't specifically about the prophetic. It was a prophetic step before the season had even looked that way to me. It brought revelation to me.

That chapter, by far, is the one people comment on as being powerfully applicable to their lives: it *speaks prophetically to **them***. But I didn't know the "work" of revelation didn't stop there. Unbeknownst to me, this response to the prophetic chapter opened the doors of heaven for all that has come since: *a new chapter for me personally*. That is a mighty move, for a life to be changed by a chapter. By God's grace, I took the risk, I trusted, and then I saw the good thing that came of it later. Obedience to God's 24/7 Voice turned me to the New Season He had in mind in the first place. That is the way God works: the unseen things move the seen.

Obedience is revelatory, it is prophetic. When we obey and *get in God's way*, we actually get out of His way: then He's free to move. It's when we second-guess, doubt, dawdle, resist, ignore, or procrastinate, that the fog settles in and we don't finish the chapter we're on. See, I needed these keys to unlock a door I didn't even know existed. I needed these keys if I wanted to proceed into the season I always knew was supposed to come. Would you like to have these keys?

Obedience Opens 3 Keys to *God's* Opportunity:

1. *Clarity* **of listening and hearing**. When we obey, we teach our spirit to listen and hear: we don't ignore and stay in *ignore*-ance. When we have obeyed, *clarity* is the blessing that proves what God's will has been all along (1 Cor. 2:14; Rom. 12:1, 2). That's when the word becomes prophetic.

2. *Determination* **to look *not* at what is visible, but at what is eternal**. I cannot see the spirit with the natural eye. Obedience is a faith move! It's on the grounds of obedience we have such confidence. (2 Cor. 4:18) Open door for prophetic fulfillment.

3. *Disconnection* **with whatever distracts**. This might be for a short season, or a more permanent thing. There's nothing worse than making a foundation for one house on two different grounds. I must stand my ground and hold God's prophetic biblical perspective in me, front and center, as the last word for my situation (Rom 12:1, 2) *That* moves the world out of the way and fulfills God's plan for me.

There's something very powerful about obeying the **clear lead of Holy Spirit** with **determination** and faith, **disconnecting** from all that tears us from this mission. *That's why there is such resistance* to the voice of God from the enemy. You hear One Voice saying, *Do this*; then you hear the enemy say, *No way, you can't, it'll be a brutal thing.* But you have to obey Holy Spirit or you won't see your next season, the *supernatural outworking* one! **He wants to open your new chapter.**

*God-seasons are not visible to the naked eye. They
are visible, alive, and moving in the Spirit*

When new chapters come into our time and space, whether personally or in world events, they fulfill something God has had waiting. Today is your appointment with God. So is tomorrow. So is the rest of the time you are here. Your appointment with God BREAKS open each new chapter in your life where you can:

- Be ready with your message
- Receive your assignment to fulfill it
- Enter the right place and time
- Activate the strategy
- Know what your chapter is called and finish it

When the Prophets and Old Testament writers wrote, **they didn't know they were writing an entire history of prophecy.** Those words were encoded, so to speak, into the rest of the text. The writers may not even have been aware of the many shifts from present into future tense and back again in their words as they wrote. They knew God was giving them something big. But how big, they had no idea! Probably a large amount of what they wrote seemed mysterious even to them. (1 Pet. 1:10–12) This multi-faceted possibility explains oftentimes why the Word seems so disjointed or hard to decipher. (Is. 7:14)

It all points out something wonderful about God's methods of communication.

The prophetic power of words:

1. Allows them to flow in the spirit, *from* the Spirit, through shifts of seasons, events, people groups (and their identities), and history itself
2. Explains why prophecy can suddenly appear, and appear fulfilled, only as it happens, has just happened, or is about to happen, in the fullness of times
3. Accounts for many prophecies having more than one fulfillment on a historical timeline: this does not detract from God's prophetic power; it establishes it further

Your new chapter might not make perfect sense yet. But hey, it's still being written! It hasn't played out yet, what can you expect? I'll *tell* you what you can expect: expect to stay with it, let God write your future, be who God says you're to be, and then you'll look back and see how it was in His hands all along!

Watch your words and make sure you really want God to perform them! Whatever God is writing on your heart, know it's not a 25-words-or-less answer. It's not simply a monologue or your 100 word bio. It is a well-crafted and epic story with chapters that begin *and* end, but not before they *lead in to what comes next*. You and God are both writing prophetically together on a tablet of heart when you speak His Word fully in faith.

"You show that you are a letter from Christ, the result of our ministry, written not with ink but with the Spirit of the living God, not on tablets of stone but on tablets of human hearts." (2 Cor. 3:3) We can't stay stuck in our last chapter when there is yet one more and one better on the way. The prophetic invitation is to begin a new chapter.

A 24/7 VOICE

Had I omitted it . . . that chapter with the prophetic word . . . what might have been different? What dream are you tempted to abort because you are hearing your own doubts more than the voice of the Spirit? Converse with God here: *mano a mano*. Use those Keys: Clarity. Determination. Disconnection from what you must, to break ties with right now . . . to connect *with* God. What things are coming clear to you these days through this practical, powerful, prophetic practice?

MANIFEST

"I have God's advantage: I know the end of our story in Christ. My Season of the Supernatural has already started. It's my chapter, opened from the Spirit for the season I'm in here on earth. I consider my life activated by Your Spirit, Your time, place, and provision, by faith. In the Name above all names, Lord Jesus."

DAY 40
YOUR 24/7 VOICE

"For we are God's masterpiece. He has created us anew in Christ Jesus, so we can do the good things he planned for us long ago." (Eph. 2:10 NLT)

Your Voice is far more than how you sound or what you say. It encompasses how you think and process ideas, how you stand, what you think is beautiful, how you word conversations and concepts, where you find meaning, and so much more. It is how you could be described. It is who you are, plus what you say and how you say it. It includes *where* you stand, what impassions and motivates you to action, the things you like to do and talk about and think on, and your priorities.

Your Voice *is* also what you say, of course. If you belong to Him it is God's voice in the earth. Regarding nothing else in creation did He say, **"Let us make human beings in our image, to be like us. They will reign** over the fish in the sea, the birds in the sky, the livestock, all the wild animals on the earth, and the small animals that scurry along the ground." (Gen. 1:26 NLT) The voice of the human being called a child of God is the single most powerful illustration of God on the face of the earth.

We are kings and queens, authorized by God to wield authority. We do that with words. The Voice, *who* we are and how we live, is the expression of our own personal footprint on earth. As we adjust our crowns for a new day, this Day 40, the question God put to me was, "What ground will your footprint take in this earth?" This fortieth day of your practical, powerful, prophetic activation is about the establishing of your Voice in the earth as God's Ambassador.

The Words and the Power

You have words of life to speak. You have health to speak over you and yours. You have salvation to speak forth to and on behalf of people, family, and nations. You are to speak to the storm. You are to take authority given to you by God and have dominion in the earth where you are. So, rise and face the challenge against His Word: believe His Word and believe His prophets and say His Word in faith, prophetically. Your heritage in Christ is to discover, apprehend, and **manifest** the wisdom of God and speak out what you hear from God's 24/7 Voice. Like the apostles did. Like the prophets, and as the followers of Jesus in every generation following have laid hold on. It's revelation that will agree with and never deny His own spoken and written Word. It will fulfill and be fulfilled.

Today the Lord says to declare over you that the prophetic power of God will settle upon you. **Your voice, your bearing,** is to be one of multitudes of ambassadors declaring HIM with prophetic intention. *Hear* this encouragement from Holy Spirit.

> Your words of the reality and ability of **God** will set free and break yokes! Who you become and what you are able to see and hear from My Spirit will speak to people you thought could not be reached. How you bear yourself will turn up the ground under them and force them to make decisions that will either save or destroy them. You will speak My word and I will work in them to do it. With no striving on your part but to remain in My words, that is how it works. Stake your claim in Me. Let your feet fall into step with Mine and your walk will be My ways, in My power, in My glory, for My glory. Worthy of a crown.
>
> Hear My 24/7 Voice. The prophetic isn't an event, it's not an action, it's not even one point in time. It is the atmosphere of the Kingdom of God, the State of the Union, immersed in Holy Spirit. Abide in Me, immersed, in the hours and season ahead. Today is the day of activation, and though it is the joy of hearts and it is a delight to hear and see from a prophetic place, the freeing up of My Spirit will also be what carries you through the tight situations coming in the next season. A new season is upon you: demand of your own heart that you will respond to Me.

From this time forth you will not simply just look at an occurrence or situation as being, "it is what it is," without asking, *God, What is this about?* You will listen for My words of explanation, discernment, wisdom, and instruction. Practice listening intently. As times grow rougher, watch carefully to see where the safe path is, what the best response is, how I can accomplish My action, who My safe contacts are, and, how I want to use you. The strategies I deliver will deliver you. This practical powerful prophetic is a lifestyle that is no longer optional. Pray in the Holy Ghost like never before.

I AM an on-time God because I **AM**. I will be where you arrive before you get there. That means the way you went and the trouble you enter will be where I have already made a way to come through. When I say I will make a path for you so you can escape, it will not be a plain path to your enemies: but it will be clear to *you.* Believe Me when I say, I AM more than enough. Today, I AM in real time with you, to impart what you need for now and later. If I take you through fire, *I AM more than the fire,* **I AM the consuming fire**, and I'll fire you up with My Spirit to go through!

If I set you before kings to give an answer to their allegations, *I AM your answer.* I tell you the truth, and it will be a creative answer no man can speak to. Allow this gift to set you free with joy! Your words will be prophetically sent to accomplish what I sent them to accomplish, for no man is beyond the power of My words.

Do not look at the person: watch Me work from the Spirit. If you meet an enemy, do not be afraid, **for I know him**, and yes, I love him. Do not fear: if you have become intimate with Me, you *will* be bold in My faith. I will cause your mouth to speak the mysteries I know about him that will catch him by Holy Spirit surprise. This is what I AM preparing for you if today you will go deeper in Me than ever before.

When the enemy comes in it will be to separate you from the pack. It will be to bring you to offenses. It will be to take the charge out of you so you are rendered inoperable. Watch for it and do not allow it for a minute, but cast it down and out in My Name. See, I have told you beforehand. Love with MY fervent, hot love that is faithful and holy!

All the treasures of wisdom and understanding will come to bear in this season and My people will rise and shine in spite of the darkness, in spite of bad news and catastrophes. For My people will stand out among the crowd: *they have been listening for My Voice alone.* My people have been watching and waiting, and now, it is time for Me to see to it that what I do next is clearly in their sites. Today, realize it: I AM healing, I AM reviving, I AM powerful on your behalf, and I AM so ready to return!

Lift up your heads. Don't say any longer, "Without Him I can do nothing," but say, "**I *have* Him!** I can do what He sends me to do; I can say what He leads me to say; I will go where He says to go BECAUSE He is with me! He is in me! My God is in my heart, and on my side, and He will come and save me, and go through with me! I am no longer a wounded warrior, but a *warrior* in a wounded world.

You have a voice. **You** *are* His voice. **You** speak His language. If you abide in Him and His words abide in you . . . you will ask what you will and it shall be done for you. (John 15:7) *That* is prophetic language! He will use **you** to reach many. This Practical Powerful Prophetic meets Thy Kingdom Come as the people of God in Christ hear the sounds of heaven. Our ears, open. Our eyes, seeing. Our hearts, His. Heaven, open to us, as He has always wanted it. Of all people **we** have been called to rule and reign through Christ. Of all people **we** can know our God and do exploits, yes, through Christ. **We're** charged with the Secrets of the Kingdom of God because we are His and we believe what He has told us. Be strong and very courageous till it "becomes you."

A 24/7 VOICE

Our life is His life, is our life. Never see yourself separated from Him again. Our spiritual DNA ("Divine Nature Activated") is at home with prophetic perception, vision, and expectation of the Kingdom of God. Our spirit "gets it"! **Pick up your pen. Prophesy to yourself throughout the days to come what God wants to see, and what you now see, and what He wants to hear, now that you hear!**

MANIFEST

"It's Time. This Manifesto is my testimony that I serve the Lord God, and He will give me a heart to know Him, that He is the

LORD. My life is in Him, and no good thing shall I lack in fulfilling my life purpose. In the Mighty Name of Jesus."

"And they shall be my people, and I will be their God: for they shall return unto me with their whole heart."

JEREMIAH 24:7

"For as many as are led by the Spirit of God, they are the sons of God. For ye have not received the spirit of bondage again to fear; but ye have received the Spirit of adoption, whereby we cry, Abba, Father. The Spirit itself bears witness with our spirit, that we are the children of God: And if children, then heirs; heirs of God, and joint-heirs with Christ; if so be that we suffer with him, that we may be also glorified together. For I reckon that the sufferings of this present time are not worthy to be compared with the glory which shall be revealed in us. For the earnest expectation of the creature waits for the manifestation of the sons of God."

ROMANS 8:14–19

APPENDIX A
JOURNALING HELPS

Over the years I've been inspired through a large assortment of journaling subjects from many sources: God's Words, books, magazine ads, conversations with people, courses I took, nature, my own healing process, circumstances and things I have seen or heard about that I ruminate on, and last but not least, the prophetic exercise of making art. Journaling puts it into a written form with Holy Spirit's insights. Look around in the situations of life you're presented with. In that large space you'll also find Holy Spirit speaking to you, 24/7.

Practice coming from God's heart of acceptance, forgiveness, building, encouragement, leading, foresight, wisdom, and yes, correction and re-direction. Seeking God is a joyful experience anytime, even when we're being gently chastised, and especially when we're aware of *our need to hear from Him* (which is pretty much, always). Journaling can go with you through the rest of your life. If you love it, it's part of the prophetic process and atmosphere your spirit lives and thrives in.

The following 40 questions, comments, and suggestions are to help prime your "heart pump" to pour out to God. The most important ingredients are your relationship with God and prayer in the Holy Ghost. Ask, seek, study, listen, see, emote, hear, connect, and write. It's prayer-time with a pen in hand.

1. Thankfulness is a powerful force, do you know why? Ponder this and write what you think and ask God for His views. Write them as if in His voice.

2. True prophecy comes from God, from within your inner man. It simply "appears" in your understanding. False prophecy comes through man's striving and "conjuring." True prophecy

builds us up in the truth and does not leave us feeling condemned, failing or rejected. Describe that difference in your own heart: what's the difference in the outcome, the way you feel after hearing each?

3. What's bothering you: In God's words to you, i.e., as if He wrote it to you right now? For instance, what does He want you to know about *fear*?

4. How does God get *your* attention? Practice today allowing Him to arrest your attention. Then write it so you will remember.

5. Write about this: "Take Your Time" . . . think first: from what vantage point will you come at it? Now speak to it, or address it. Is it about taking time captive? Or is it my time I should be *taking*, and not thinking it is just 24 hours that belong to no one?

6. What's your biggest hindrance to exercising the prophetic? Do a Bible search and locate the prophetic in action.

7. Which fruit of the Spirit is most powerful to you at this time in your life? Why? What *events* can you associate with what God is showing you?

8. What encouragement would God give you in a time of loneliness? If you've never been lonely, write about why you think this blessing has been yours.

9. How would you encourage someone to step out into their gifting? What would God say through you? And does He speak that same grace to you?

10. Think of three insights you have had about the prophetic from this book.

11. The word *humble* means *teachable*. Are you humble? Name some ways. Are you teachable? What does God say He can do with who you are? Write it as if God is speaking it to you.

12. Write about something you have learned recently that you are sure came from Holy Spirit . . . something you noticed,

or heard, or about which you thought and have come to an interesting observation.

13. What did you see in nature recently that caught your attention? What did it "say" to you? How does that help your personal perspective?

14. Write a prayer to God inspired by something in His Word. You can change the wording to a *simple prophetic statement* by adjusting the way it is worded. Example: Your prayer is, "I want to love people around me better because love is of God and everyone who loves is born of God and knows God." (1 John 4:7, 8) Prayerfully remembering that *His own words are prophetic and will accomplish what they are sent to do*, this can be said to be a prophetic response from God to you: "Child, how I love you! I have poured out My love to you, and I have love for *you* to pour out, because I have poured out My love *in* you. You are going to know Me so much better when this becomes a river of life in you." This is wisdom and understanding coming forth that turns the *logos* of the Word to a *rhema*, alive word, as it bubbles up while you ruminate on it! Often I hear Him take it one more step into action: "Are you ready to go with Me here, to the giving place?"

15. Write about childlike trust or any other subject you're in need of. Is it different from where you feel like you are presently? Ask God to speak to you about what He wants to do in you to free you to trust completely. An acrostic often helps here. Use any form you feel led to, I use the word **trust** here because it just made sense. Your acrostic of trust would be different and formed for you, by Holy Spirit and you working together:

> **T**hanking You for always being here
> **R**emembering You are who You say You are
> **U**nloading my cares because You care for me
> **S**itting still and knowing I am safe with You
> **T**aking my time to listen

16. God is deliberately at work in your life. Always. Describe how that makes you feel about Him. About yourself.

17. Use your favorite verse to "illustrate" how God feels about the subject. Use words, pictures, colors, cut-outs, etc.

18. "What's on your mind, God?" In God's words to you, i.e., as if He wrote it to you right now: what does He want you to know? No condemnation, only building up.

19. Seeking God is a joyful experience even when we're being re-directed. Write about a time this comment reminds you of.

20. Do certain things intimidate you? From God's Word, what would He say to you about this? Be brave and list ten things He would say to you!

21. What are your main three prayer requests right now? Write them out and find scripture that helps you.

22. Write a personal observation of your choice: "It's easy for me to always be thinking about sowing and giving. But I sometimes don't feel worthy to reap a good thing. What could be going on in my heart?" Your thoughts on the matter, Lord? What needs to happen?

23. Grace is a powerful force. Describe it as best you can, and ask God for revelation of it in your life from this day forward.

24. Write about this again: "Take Your Time" . . . think first: from what vantage point did I come at it the *first* time? Now speak to it, or address it, it another way, from another viewpoint. And if not this phrase, is there another one that sparks your thoughts?

25. Think of someone you know who's going through a difficult time. Read Psalm 23 and use those images to prayerfully tell your friend who God is for him or her. This is the testimony of Jesus, the spirit of prophecy: His words are meant for us to hear and believe. Go ahead and *prophesy* (speak it out in faith before they have it operating in them) to this person and say, *I do believe the Lord means for you to know this, because it is your heritage. . . .*

26. What do you need to see or know to get beyond the immediate difficulty of your own life?

27. Sowing life to the Spirit means a rich harvest. What good things would you most like to see come to you? Ask God what it will take.

28. What's bothering you: does it feel like something has gotten in the way of the intimacy you have had with God in times past, even recently? Ask God to take you back to what moved in to obstruct your vision of Him. Write it down, then pray and believe if He opened it up for you to understand then consider it taken care of by faith. His Word (the Bible) is Truth.

29. What did you *hear* recently that caught your attention? What did it "look like" to you? How does this change your perspective? How are seeing and hearing so often interchangeable, anyway?

30. Write about the word, *harvest*. If you can find a neat picture, glue it in the journal page to inspire you. I hope you are cutting and pasting all over this personal journal: creativity will help the right side of your brain to grow confident and strong, and that is where the prophetic comes through in power.

31. Keep an eye out for advertising slogans: so many of these words meant to "get our attention" are potentially prophetic words for us to hear and see things of the Spirit. Cut out a few. Don't misunderstand: I'm not seeking and don't want the world's opinion, I want *His*! But many prophetic ideas come forth because creatively used words are containers for spirit.

32. Aha! Words are containers for spirit. How? Why? What do you want to do with them? By the way, what does the word *"contain"* say to you? Do a word search in the Bible and make sure this concept is actually scriptural. It'll change your life.

33. Repentance is a powerful force. Try an acrostic using the letters of the word and fill in with **Benefits of living a life of Repentance**.

34. What is "good ground" of the heart? Describe it and describe what can grow in it.

35. Ask God to give you wisdom about how to reach your neighbors better. If there are problems there, ask God for His prophetic solutions and ideas. He wants to reach them. Write out your next thoughts.

36. If you have asked God for help in an area, how will this change help you in the next months to live closer to Him?

37. When you go through a difficult thing, what is the hardest part of it? Ask God to speak to this point, speak to you though His Spirit, in your journal.

38. Write about this: "I bless you in the Name of Jesus."

39. Write a prayer to God inspired by something in His Word. You can change the wording to a *simple prophetic statement*

by adjusting the way it is worded. Using the pattern from #14, do this exercise again. Realizing that Christ Jesus lives in our hearts by faith and that He wants to commune with us 24/7, words that you think in line with scripture are already prophetic. Why not recognize them to be and accept them as yours. The purpose is for *all He is* to spring up from God's own words to make it *come alive in you.*

40. Write about the future: what's happening in America or your country; how does it tie into the larger prophetic story unfolding? This is a large subject but you surely have thoughts on it. Who and what is God directing you to become in these days? Put God as the speaker.

APPENDIX B
ACROSTIC PSALMING

This is about one of my favorite times with the Lord in worship and fellowship. It's something *you* can do even if you never have, and practicing will expand your ease with words. You can talk to God, listen for His words, or pour out some theme that is strong in your heart or that you want to be a stronger theme. It is communicating with God in your language with Him. It's the way David wrote many of his psalms.

As you write to a "grid" that helps you remember the words you need and want to use, you'll find that you can pour out your words better to God in prayer as well. I use acrostics to worship, to pray and praise, to think through situations and ask for His guidance, to mourn and wait for His reply. And sometimes to complain. Okay, I admitted it. God often responds *through* His Spirit *in* me, in much the same way as He did with David. The beauty and benefit of Acrostic Psalms is they are easier to remember because they're written in a mnemonic (memorable) style.

In Psalm 119, the longest psalm, the psalmist used a letter of the alphabet to begin every stanza in its section. For example, the first eight lines begin with the letter *aleph*. That section is titled, *Aleph*. The next eight lines begin with the second letter of the alphabet, *Beth*. The third section begins with *Gimel*, and you guessed it, each line begins with that letter. All the way through this psalm. It would be like writing a poem using the letter B for the Poem, "Be"

Before I awake every morning I
Bring a sacrifice of praise to You.
Beginning my day with You in first place
Blesses not only You, God,
But me!

This is a practical way to learn how to prophesy because it frees you to not feel too rigid about how you can word something. Pray in the Spirit. Read the Word and think about it. Make faith declarations based on His Word for what you are praying. When I wrote this, below, I was thinking about our assured victory even when all we are doing at the moment is *professing* our victory. Do a Psalm search and find the many psalms that use this same format of **changing the person who is peaking**. That's because it is a conversation between us and our Lord. This exercise should help you understand areas where that is happening in scripture. Here's how to read it: what started the poem was my **rehearsing God's blessings** and provision to you and me. Then it turned to my words being spoken **to God in prayer**, at "O". Then at the end of "W" where the quote begins with, "Reflect," it was **the Holy Spirit speaking to me** and us! I put those words in quotes.

AN ACROSTIC PSALM ABOUT GOD'S ECONOMY

Announce this good news to your brothers and sisters: *here* is our heritage:
Binding and loosing begins on earth and ends in heaven, as we
Call those things which be not as though they are, then *heaven* brings it to pass!
Death cannot hold us because
Eternity is written in our hearts already, automatically, by the work of God our
Father. Father! Father
God! Whose words become our words, whose ways become our ways.
He's making us to be like Him, right inside our heart! He's making us
Imitators of God: yes, we can do all things through
Jesus, in His anointing that strengthens the weak and weary.
Kings and priests are who we are, chosen to rule and reign with our
Lord on earth; and we get to begin this
Magnificent calling
Now, today!
***Our* offerings of praise are *Yours*, God!**

Powerful because of Your Blood; our prayers are heard because
    You have us in Your heart. Alleluia!
Questions we raise are answered in a resounding Yes! Amen! Be-
    cause You
Ran rough shod over the enemy, and now our
Steps are ordered so we walk in Your ways. You get the glory, Lord!
The tables are turned over so we need never be caged and stuck
Under the thumb of the enemy. Unparalleled favor, unmatched
Victory is assured before the battle begins, because of You, our
    God! We
Win and we reign in life by One, and Only, Christ Jesus! **"Reflect
on these things** and
eXpect your victory; *expect* **My** Spirit to move in power and answer
You in every difficult place! For when your expectation is of Me it is
    My
Zeal that will accomplish it!"

This prophetic practice can serve you well for the rest of your life
and bless many people. They can turn into music beautifully if you're
so inclined. You may feel led to write one for someone, or Holy Spirit
may say this one is to be read to the church as a group activation
(submit to authorities first). Or you can practice using scriptures that
start with that particular letter.

A new commandment I give you: because I love you
Bring your tithes to the storehouse: because I love you
Cast your cares upon Me: because I love you

Each time you are recalling the Word, you see, it is establishing it
in your heart! Do you remember the acronym for GRACE? Once you
hear it, you'll probably always remember it:

God's
Riches
At
Christ's
Expense

Now I want to suggest that in a time, hopefully never, or hopefully far out from here and now, if you ever are without a Bible, that *you still have a new song and psalm in your heart.* I have an imagination, and I am imagining now a brother or sister in prison. **No Bible allowed.** Actually nothing in that prison cell but a **torn filthy blanket.** After some brutal sleep deprivation, your mind feels too weary for recall; but in your heart, with a grid of bars (ABCs or a word to use as a grid) in front of you, out of your belly flow rivers of living water from Holy Spirit! The bars are not the main thing; but the grid they offer allows you to flow with the supply of heaven. Ironic, right? They can be a praise, an encouragement to one or many, or a lament; they can voice the Gospel or send a message. Part of our ruling and reigning heritage is a practical powerful prophetic way of *living in any circumstances.*

> Blanket, O lord, this space
> Live over me, speak and prophesy over me here
> And be the glory and the lifter of my head.
> Near me. That's where you are, my
> King and Redeemer. Your robes of glory and righteousness
> Ever cover me, comfort me, and keep me
> Tightly in Your wrap.

When the left side of our brain is fatigued or even damaged, the right side comes to the fore. Today, bless the right side of your brain by taking it out for a spin.

APPENDIX C
WHAT TO DO WITH PERSONAL PROPHECY

Many people hear from God over the years about things they were called to become, develop, and do. Sometimes, in the course of time as they waited for God to do this wonderful thing, the dream got hazy and farther away than when they received it. Then, because they didn't *know* what to do with it, know where to turn for discernment or direction, they let it fall away to time and circumstance.

Most callings are miraculous, let's face it. When we hear a prophetic word it's the best thing we ever heard! (Or maybe not, but because you know you heard from Him, it is a consolation) God knows my name? My life means something? He wants to use me? He would stoop that low to work in me and through me? The answer is, *yes, and so be it.* Now for the real miracle: making it happen. Whose job is that? It's not a trick question.

Different churches and organizations have different criteria for judging personal prophecies, but all had these basics. I assembled these from three sources, Kenneth Copeland Ministries, Christian International's Apostle Bill Hamon, and The Prophetic Institute at House of Faith, Inc. The idea is accountability so no one moves on or gets comfortable until it is certain that Holy Spirit has spoken.

WHAT TO DO WITH PERSONAL PROPHECY, DREAMS AND VISIONS

10 Vital Pre-Birth Measures for Prophetic Fulfillment

The best place to be when receiving a personal prophetic word is in the company of trusted, believing prayer warriors when you receive any word. But this isn't always possible. We are not always in the company of prophetically aware believers who want to see you reach the blessing God is holding out for you. For that matter, you could be almost anywhere: in a field, on a treadmill, in your room, on a plane, swimming, at the dentist. The following steps will help you to not only let the word of personal prophecy be tested to "see if these things be so," but to help you lean into Holy Spirit and allow the Body of Christ to be part of this interaction in the Spirit, for your safety. No one lives in a vacuum, especially the parts of Christ's own body. God is invested in you from (before) your birth. Believe He will be faithful to complete what He started in you:

1. Hear the prophetic word. Let it sink in. In that moment, cast the care of this word (as in *taking care of it*) on the Lord. He can handle it and will help you.

2. Receive this word in the Name of Jesus, by faith. Proclaim it right there: "I receive this in the Name of Jesus!" Is it an impossibility? Good. That means *He* must accomplish, with your cooperation.

3. Write it down so you can see it again and again. Consider it in your heart and lay it on the altar. Keep a journal to keep all you discover in one place and take it with you when you go; or make sure you enter the word in your journal later.

4. Speak it back out of your mouth! Speak it to yourself as often as you need, to cast down the negatives you've said so often.

5. Submit the word to prophetically aware believers: your pastors, prophets in the church, trusted mentors. They need to be people skillful in the Word and the prophetic, mature believers who want to *see you reach the blessing God is holding out for you.* They also care enough about you to urge you not to head in a direction unprepared or ill-advised. Sit and submit to their wisdom and take it to the Lord in prayer: it's part of your preparation and growth.

6. Learn all you can about the type of situation this word calls you to: ministry, mission, marketplace development, teaching,

written or spoken subjects. Begin to order your ways to head in that direction, all the while giving God permission to lead and perform His works on your behalf.

7. Thank God every time you think of it! He is faithful to perform it. Remind your mind of His Word that is so full of hope and help. Write those verses down with the word you have received to "judge" (assess) it all in the light of God's alive Word.

8. Sow spiritual seed toward this word of promise: invest something of yourself into it and into areas God directs you to: time, helps, funds, prayer, talents, etc. The operative word is GIVE.

9. Wait for it. Expect it, as long as it takes. Expect till your enemies be made your footstool (the enemy of your soul doesn't want you to get fired up about the fulfillment of the testimony of Jesus Christ in you!).

10. Guard your heart; when you become sure of this word's accuracy, you'll find some in your company are not into it. Be careful who you hang out with in this process. Someone who dismisses your heart-cry may not be the friend you want to spend hours with right now.

A prophetic caution: If you hear a word for someone else you feel is from Holy Spirit and want to give it to them, write it and follow the advice in #5 for their benefit and your safety. Before it reaches your friend. You can see how necessary it is to be in a strong and mature church of entire-Bible-believing, five-fold ministry brothers and sisters who flow in the prophetic.

APPENDIX D
RESOURCES AND RECOMMENDED READING

Prophetic events, discoveries, developments and fulfillments are unfolding on a daily basis. If you want to know where we stand on a prophetic timeline for the world, there are plenty of helps for someone who wants to pursue to the "end of the story." I've included sources that speak to these issues and encourage you to explore, but with the understanding that it will be your own private relationship with Holy Spirit that will keep you in these times, not the information you gather in these sites. I see them as fascinating, Word corroborating, prepper materials; but I see God's Word as my life and salvation. If all this *supernatural* and *prophetic* begins to consume you to the exclusion of the Word being first place in life, then adjust your trajectory (repent) and *get back in the Word*, with a newly informed appreciation for His truth.

Everyone has a slightly different prophetic footprint because we're created for a specific communication of Christ Jesus. My prophetic footprint includes activating the Church in the prophetic; eschatology and end time prophecy; and the prophetic Fine Arts in prophetic worship and ministry, and in its mission of communicating Christ in our culture. The sources I site below are a mix of these areas of interest.

Search out Christian sources. NASA was scientifically helpful regarding blood moons and the like. A few sources I've shared in regards to the arts can help if this is your area of interest. By and large, names like Jonathan Cahn, James Goll, John Ankerberg, Hal Lindsey, John Hagee, Perry Stone, Sid Roth, Gary Stearman, Apostle Bill Hamon, and many more have proven tried and true over the decades, and are available online in a large assortment of prophetic categories.

Barton, David. http://www.wallbuilders.com/

Blackstone, William E. *Jesus is Coming: God's Hope for a Restless World*. Grand Rapids: Kregel Communications. 1989.

Blanchard, Ken and Hodges, Phil. *Lead Like Jesus: Lessons from the Greatest Leadership Role Model of All Time*. Nashville: Thomas Nelson, Inc. 2005.

http://www.breakingisraelnews.com/

http://www.charismamag.com/

http://www.christianaid.org/

http://www.christianinternational.com

http://civa.org/ Christians in the Visual Arts.

Coffee, Jacque. *Your Gung-Ho! Life: The ABCs of Proactive Living*. Spring Hill, FL: Jumping Canvas Press. 2012.

Cooke, Graham. *Approaching the Heart of Prophecy: A Journey into Encouragement, Blessing, and Prophetic Gifting*. Winston-Salem, NC: Punch Press. 2006.

Copeland, Kenneth. *The Blessing of the Lord: Makes Rich and He Adds No Sorrow With It: Proverbs 10:22*. Fort Worth: Kenneth Copeland Ministries. 2011.

Edwards, Betty. *Drawing From the Right Side of the Brain: A Course in Enhancing Creativity and Artistic Confidence*. Los Angeles: Jeremy P. Tarcher, Inc. 1989.

http://www.elshaddaiministries.us/

Kendall, R.T. *Holy Fire: A Balanced, Biblical Look at the Holy Spirit's Work in our Lives*. Lake Mary, FL: Charisma House. 2014.

Parshall, Janet. http://www.moodyradio.org/in-the-market-with-janet-parshall/

https://prophecywatchers.com

Roth, Sid. www.SidRoth.org. *It's Supernatural! And Messianic Vision*.

Sheets, Dutch. *The River of God: Moving in the Flow of God's Plan for Revival*. Ventura: Renew: a Division of Gospel Light. 1998.

Smith, Laura Harris. *Seeing the Voice of God: What God is Telling You through Dreams & Visions.* Minneapolis, MN: Chosen Books. 2014.

https://stream.org/

Stone. Perry. Manna-Fest: Perry Stone Ministries

www.rapturewatch.net/apps/videos

Richardson, Joel. *The Islamic Anti-Christ: The Shocking Truth about the Real Nature of the Beast.* Los Angeles: WND Books. 2009.

https://trunews.com

Veith, Gene Edward, Jr. *Postmodern Times: A Christian Guide to Contemporary Thought and Culture.* Wheaton, IL: Crossway Books. 1994.

Virkler, Mark and Patti. *4 Keys to Hearing God's Voice.* PA: Destiny Image Publishers, Inc. 2010.

http://www.persecution.com/ Voice of the Martyrs

Wurmbrand, Richard. *Tortured for Christ, 30th Anniversary Edition.* Bartlesville, OK: Living Sacrifice Book Co. 1998.

.

ABOUT THE AUTHOR

Jacque Coffee is passionate to see people *gung-ho!* about God and hearing His 24/7 voice to experience deeper, stronger, and yes, prophetic relationship with Him.

Her teaching, writing, and art stir up creative, communicative empowerment for the Church. Her first book, *Your Gung-Ho! Life, The ABCs of Proactive Living* (with workbook), encourages all-out, Holy Spirit-energized ways of living, with personal choices taking on the significance they deserve. It's the perfect first step to her second book you now hold in your hands.

As a working artist and designer, Coffee has extensive and varied experience: fine art painting, furniture design, showroom and interior design; a co-owner and designer of companies manufacturing furniture, accessories, and store signage; faux-finish artist, craft design, and book illustration; home staging, renovation, visual merchandising, set design; even designing a home addition on an 1800s log home. Early in her walk in Christ, it was a natural fit to head into *prophetic art*. This was "interior" design at its best, and became her first ministry form.

Forty plus years into Christ, tens of thousands of hours studying, teaching, coaching, and most recently as an author and pastor, Jacque has impacted several generations with gung-ho! devotion, wake-up calls, and an encouragement factor straight from God. Her prophetic message, art, and books are time-sensitive wake-up calls for today's Church, with *This Practical Powerful Prophetic: 40 Days to Hearing God's 24/7 Voice* being the most concise intro yet into God's creative, prophetic announcement of the Kingdom.

Pastor Jacque holds a MA in Theological Studies, Christian Ministries, and is a Licensed Minister through Christian International Apostolic Ministries at House of Faith in Hudson, Florida. With a prophetic gift to sense the season and the need, she "pours out" in speaking, ministry venues, and conducting prophetic art workshops.

For additional information or to contact Jacque Coffee, visit her at:

https://www.JacqueCoffee.com

https://www.linkedin.com/pub/jacque-coffee/

https://www.facebook.com/Jacque-Coffee-heres-to-Your-Gung-Ho-Life

CPSIA information can be obtained
at www.ICGtesting.com
Printed in the USA
LVOW04s2236081115

461595LV00002B/8/P